The
Canadian
EDIBLE
GARDEN

Vegetables, Herbs, Fruits & Seeds

Alison Beck

LONE
PINE

Lone Pine Publishing

The Publisher: Lone Pine Publishing
10145–81 Avenue
Edmonton, AB
T6E 1W9
Canada
Website: www.lonepinepublishing.com

Library and Archives Canada Cataloguing in Publication

Beck, Alison, 1971-
    The Canadian edible garden / Alison Beck.

Includes bibliographical references and index.
ISBN 978-1-55105-579-4

    1. Gardening--Canada. 2. Plants, Edible—Canada. 3. Vegetable gardening—Canada. I. Title.

SB451.36.C3B43 2007   635.0971   C2007-906017-X

Editorial Director: Nancy Foulds
Editorial: Wendy Pirk
Photo Coordinator: Carol Woo
Production Manager: Gene Longson
Book Design, Layout & Production: Heather Markham
Cartography: Mike Cooke
Cover Design: Gerry Dotto
Photographs: page 248

The frost free days map (p. 8) and the hardiness map (p. 9) were adapted from *The Atlas of Canada* (http://atlas.gc.ca) © 2008. Produced under licence from Her Majesty the Queen in Right of Canada, with permission of Natural Resources Canada.

We acknowledge the financial support of the Government of Canada through the Book Publishing Industry Development Program (BPIDP) for our publishing activities.

PC: P15

Contents

Introduction

Edible gardens have been part of human culture for thousands of years. Along with harnessing fire, developing the wheel and domesticating animals, cultivating food is one of the benchmarks of human advancement. Growing plants that provide food and learning to store it for times of scarcity were advancements that allowed humans to develop civilizations.

When we buy food from the grocery store, we give little thought to where it came from, how far it had to travel and how much it cost to transport it, first to the store and then to the table. We don't think about how it was grown or who grew it. When we grow our own food plants, we develop a greater appreciation for the food, our gardens and our own ability to provide for ourselves and our families.

An edible garden includes much more than just vegetables. There is a multitude of edible fruits, seeds, flowers and herbs that thrive in our gardens. From adding a few favourites to patio containers and borders to designing an entire landscape with edibles, the possibilities are endless.

There are many good reasons to grow edible plants. You can save money on your grocery bill; it's environmentally friendly because fewer resources will be used growing and getting the food to your table; it saves wildlife habitat by reducing the need to expand cultivated land; it gives you a chance to seek out varieties and specialty items; and an often-overlooked reason to grow edible plants is that they are attractive and often unique in appearance.

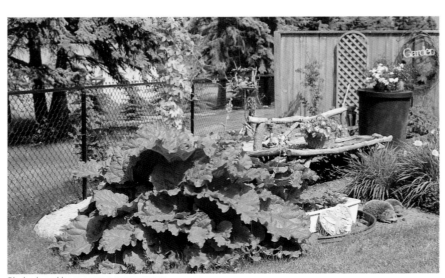

Rhubarb and hops grace a sunny corner.

can be added to the landscape you already have. They don't have to be planted in rows; single plants and small groups can make attractive features. Also, if you do not plant a single type of plant in one location, pest and disease problems are less likely to affect your entire crop.

Think about your favourite vegetables and fruits. You don't have to try to accommodate your food needs for an entire year, but you could supplement what you buy by growing a few plants. Do you eat a lot of broccoli? Three to six plants can provide two people with a lot of meals because many selections produce additional smaller heads once the main one is cut. A container of tomatoes combined with flowering annuals on a sunny balcony or deck is beautiful and functional. Four zucchini plants will leave you wondering what to do with all your extra zucchini.

Canada is an ideal place to grow a huge variety of edible plants. Many of our favourites like to grow in a climate where summer temperatures are moderate and the days are long. Some edible plants grow equally well in all parts of Canada, but each region provides a niche in which a select few excel.

Many gardeners are put off by the thought of digging up a square or rectangle and having an uninspiring display of rows in their carefully landscaped garden. Edible gardening doesn't have to be this way. Plenty of edible plants

Overall, Canada is a fantastic country in which to garden, though the cold winter weather and potentially short growing season in many regions do present some challenges. A wealth of diverse growing conditions are found here—almost every imaginable gardening situation short of tropical is experienced somewhere in the country. The adjacent oceans significantly modify the climate on both the East Coast and the West Coast, resulting in more moderate winter temperatures and cooler summers, as well as fog, salty air and, often, thin, rocky, acidic soils.

Warm summers and cold winters dominate in most of eastern and central Canada and the climate is modified by the regions' proximity to water. The floodplains that border the St. Lawrence River are fertile and deep. Gardeners on the Canadian Shield generally have acidic and fertile but rocky soils, whereas those living around Georgian Bay and the Great Lakes may have sandy or rocky soils. Southern Ontario has mostly alkaline, less rocky soil and milder winters, thanks to the moderating effect of the Great Lakes.

The cold winters of the Prairies are hard on tender perennial plants, but the sun-filled days of summer encourage plant growth. The soils can be clay, sand or loam, and they tend to be alkaline.

The Rocky Mountains have short, often dry summers and cold winters. The valleys between the mountains are often more temperate, and there is no shortage of gardeners to take advantage of the best the region has to offer. The North, though sparsely populated, has its share of determined gardeners as well. The varied geography shares many

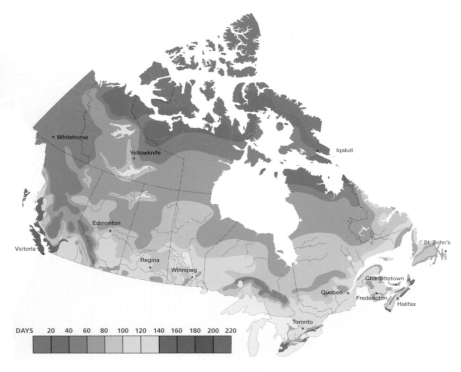

DAYS   20   40   60   80   100   120   140   160   180   200   220

Frost Free Days Map

traits with adjacent areas farther south, such as the Rockies or the Prairies, but typically with thin, acidic soils, low levels of precipitation, scattered permafrost, very cold winters and a short growing season.

Despite these regional characteristics and limitations, conditions can deviate greatly from garden to garden within a region. In addition to broad factors such as climate, season length and day length, the details of soil conditions, garden microclimates, light and heat influence your garden regardless of where you are in Canada. These can vary not only from garden to garden but within a single garden.

The three most important pieces of climate information for Canadian gardeners are the hardiness zone, the last

Hardiness Zones Map

frost date of spring and the first frost date of fall. These are not hard and fast rules but are excellent guidelines that will help you pick plants and plan your garden. Hardiness zones (see map, above) are relevant mostly for perennials, trees and shrubs. Plants are rated based on the hardiness zone they will grow in. The frost dates are a good estimate of season length (see map, p. 8). If you can only depend on four frost-free months, you may want to choose plants that will survive a light frost or that will mature during your anticipated growing season.

This information provides a good starting point but should not completely rule your planting decisions. An early, warm spring is an excellent opportunity to set a few plants out early, while a cold, wet, late spring might mean waiting a week or two more than you expected.

As with any gardening, growing edible plants should be fun. They can add unique colours and textures to your garden and your dinner plate. Experiment with a few each year, and you may find yourself looking for space to add even more.

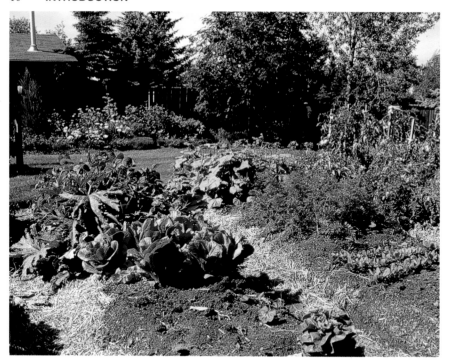

Edibles in the Garden

Edible gardens come in many forms and include a wide variety of plants. The neat rows of a traditional Canadian vegetable garden were adopted from the farm garden, and the attention paid to plant and row spacing is designed to make large numbers of plants more easily accessible. If you have plenty of space and want loads of vegetables to store over winter, this style can work for you and is still preferred by many gardeners.

There is no need to segregate edible plants from ornamental ones. The French *potager*, or kitchen garden, is a garden that is both decorative and functional. It generally consists of a symmetrical arrangement of raised beds. Plants are often repeated in a location in the bed rather than having one bed of all the same plant. Vegetables are combined with herbs and fruiting shrubs as well as edible flowers.

In intensive gardens, plantings are made in groups rather than rows. They may be formal or informal. An example of a more formal intensive garden is a square-foot garden. A square raised bed measuring 120 cm (48") along each side is divided into 16 smaller planting squares. Each square is planted with as much of a single crop as the space will allow. As soon as a crop has matured and been harvested, something new is planted to replace it as long as the growing season allows.

An informal intensive garden could resemble a cottage-style garden, with vegetables planted in groups and drifts throughout the beds. Tucking groups of

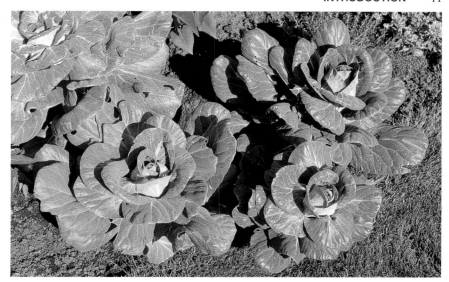

vegetables into existing beds could be formal or informal, depending on the nature of the garden you have.

There are many options for gardeners with limited gardening space. Many of the fruits, vegetables and herbs we enjoy grow successfully in containers on a balcony, porch or deck. If you don't have room for trailing vines to spread, consider a trellis or obelisk and have the vines grow up instead of out. Many of the same vine forming plants you can grow up trellises will also trail nicely over the edge of a hanging basket.

As your garden grows and develops and you need to add new plants, think about adding edible ones. If you need a new shrub, perhaps you could include a raspberry or blueberry bush; asparagus, fiddlehead fern and rhubarb are hardy perennial choices; and the wealth of annual options is nearly limitless.

Ornamental Value

The ornamental value of edible plants is too often overlooked. Edible plants vary in size, colour and texture and often have wonderful flowers, stunning foliage or decorative fruit in colours and shapes not often replicated in our ornamental plants. When you look at an edible plant, don't just think about the end result; think about the appearance of the plant and what it can add to your ornamental garden.

When planting intensively, keep plants fairly close together but leave enough room for each to grow and spread. Many edibles grow from small seedlings into large mature plants very quickly, and your yield will be greatly reduced if plants don't have at least some room to spread.

Artichoke (above), amaranth (centre), red cabbage (below)

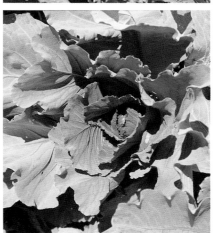

Many edible plants have stunning foliage. Their leaves come in a wide range of colours, from bloomy grey-green and greens so dark they're almost black to shades of red, purple, yellow, blue and bronze. Some foliage is patterned or has veins that contrast with the colour of the leaves. Foliage can be immense or delicate and feathery.

Edibles with Interesting Foliage
Amaranth
Artichoke
Asparagus
Cabbage
Carrots
Chard
Coriander
Fennel
Fiddlehead Ferns
Kale
Leeks
Lettuce
Mustard
Rhubarb
Squash

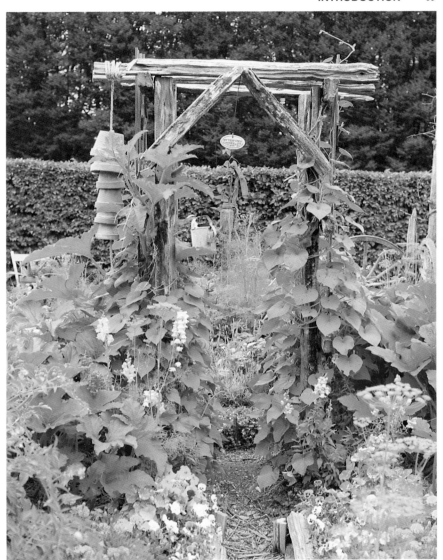

Getting Started

Finding the right edibles for your garden requires experimentation and creativity. Before you start planting, consider the growing conditions in your garden; these conditions will influence not only the types of plants you select, but also the location in which you plant them. Plants will be healthier and less susceptible to problems if grown in optimum conditions. It is difficult to significantly modify most of your garden's existing conditions; an easier approach is to match the plants to the garden.

Your plant selection will be influenced by the levels of light and amount of exposure in your garden; the porosity, pH and texture of the soil; the amount of exposure in your garden; and the plants' tolerance to frost. Sketching your garden may help you visualize how various conditions might affect your planting decisions. Note shaded areas, low-lying or wet areas, exposed or windy sections, etc. Understanding your garden's growing conditions will help you learn where plants will perform best and prevent you from making costly mistakes in your planning.

Light

There are four basic levels of light in a garden: full sun, partial shade (partial sun), light shade and full shade. Buildings, trees, fences and the position of the sun at different times of the day and year affect available light. Knowing what light is available in your garden will help you determine where to place each plant.

Plants in full sun locations, such as along south-facing walls, receive more than six hours of direct sunlight during the day. Locations classified as partial shade, such as east- or west-facing walls, receive direct sunlight for part of the day (four to six hours) and shade for the rest. Light shade locations receive shade for most or all of the day, although some sunlight does filter through to ground level. An example of a light shade location might be the ground under a small-leaved tree such as a birch. Full shade locations, which can include the north side of a house, receive no direct sunlight.

Plant your edibles where they will grow best. If your garden has hot, dry areas or low-lying, damp sections, select plants that prefer those conditions. Experimenting will help you learn about the conditions of your garden.

Raised bed in full sun

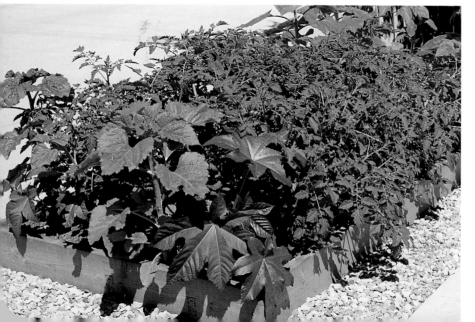

Soil

Soil quality is an extremely important element of a healthy garden. Plant roots rely on the air, water and nutrients that are held within the soil. Of course, plants also depend on soil to hold them upright. The soil in turn benefits from plant roots breaking down large clumps while preventing erosion by binding together small particles and by reducing the amount of exposed surface. When plants die and break down, they add organic nutrients to soil and feed beneficial microorganisms.

Soil is made up of particles of different sizes. Sand particles are the largest—water drains quickly from sandy soil and nutrients tend to get washed away. Sandy soil does not compact very easily because the large particles leave air pockets between them. Clay particles, which are the smallest, can be seen only through a microscope. Clay holds the most nutrients, but it also compacts easily and has little air space. Clay is slow to absorb water and equally slow to let it drain. Silt is midway between sand and clay in particle size. Most soils are a combination of these three particles and are called loams.

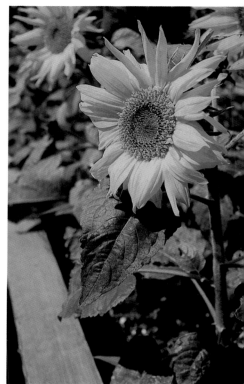

Sunflowers tolerate a range of soil conditions (above); chard (below) is one of the few vegetables that tolerates light shade.

It is important to consider the pH level (the scale on which acidity or alkalinity is measured) of soil, which influences the availability of nutrients. Most plants thrive in soil with a pH between 5.5 and 7.5. Soil pH varies a great deal from place to place in Canada. Testing kits can be purchased at most garden centres, and soil-testing labs can analyze the pH and the quantities of various nutrients in your soil. The acidity of soil can be reduced with the addition of horticultural lime or wood ashes and increased with the addition of sulphur, peat moss or pine needles. For plants that prefer a pH that varies greatly from that of your garden soil, use planters or create raised beds where it is easier to control and alter the pH level of soil.

Water drainage is affected by soil type and the terrain in your garden. Plants that prefer well-drained soil and do not require a large amount of moisture grow well on a sloping hillside garden with rocky soil. Water retention in these areas can be improved through the addition of organic matter. Plants that thrive on a consistent water supply or in boggy conditions are ideal for low-lying areas that retain water for longer periods or that hardly drain at all. In extremely wet areas, you can improve drainage by adding gravel, creating raised beds or using French drains or drainage tile.

Exposure

Your garden is exposed to wind, heat, cold and rain, and some plants are better adapted than others to withstand the potential damage of these forces. Buildings, walls, fences, hills, hedges, trees and even tall perennials influence and often reduce exposure.

Wind and heat are the most likely elements to cause damage. The sun can be very intense, and heat can rise quickly on a sunny afternoon. Choose edibles that tolerate or even thrive in hot weather in your garden's hot spots.

Too much rain can damage plants, as can over-watering. Early in the season, a light mulch will help prevent seeds or seedlings from being washed away in heavy rain. Later, most established plants beaten down by heavy rain will recover, but some are slow to do so. Waterlogged soil can encourage root rot

Open spaces expose plants to stronger wind.

because many edible plants prefer well-drained soil.

Hanging moss-lined baskets are susceptible to wind and heat exposure, losing water from the soil surface and the leaves. Hanging baskets look wonderful, but watch for wilting, and water the baskets regularly to keep them looking great. New water-holding polymers that hold water and release it as the soil dries have been developed for use in soil mixes.

Frost Tolerance

When planting edibles, consider their ability to tolerate an unexpected frost. Most Canadian gardeners can expect a chance of frost until mid- to late May, though warmer areas may have a last frost date in April and colder areas in June. The map on p. 8 gives a general idea of when you can expect your last frost date. Your local garden centre should be able to provide more precise information on frost expectations for your area.

Mulch (above)

Edible plants are grouped into three categories based on how tolerant they are of cold weather: hardy, half-hardy or tender.

Hardy plants can tolerate low temperatures and even frost. They can be planted in the garden early and may survive long into autumn or even winter. These plants often fade in the heat of summer after producing an early crop. Many hardy edibles are sown directly in the garden in the weeks before the last frost date and can be sown again in summer for a second autumn crop.

Half-hardy plants can tolerate a light frost but will be killed by a heavy one. These edibles can be planted out around the last frost date and will generally benefit from being started indoors from seed if they are slow to mature.

Tender plants have no frost tolerance at all and might suffer even if the temperatures drop to a few degrees above freezing. These plants are often started early indoors and are not planted in the garden until the last frost date has passed and the ground has had a chance to warm up. The advantage is that these edibles are often tolerant of hot summer temperatures.

Protecting plants from frost is relatively simple. Cover plants overnight with sheets, towels, burlap or even cardboard boxes—don't use plastic because it doesn't provide any insulation.

Kale tolerates freezing temperatures (above). Lettuce tolerates light frost, while nasturtiums are quickly killed by cold (below).

Peas prefer cold weather and will tolerate spring frosts.

Choosing the type of edibles to grow is just the beginning. There are often dozens of selections of some of our favourites. Choose plants and cultivars that are suitable to the climate and conditions in your garden. For example, avoid pumpkin that needs four or five months to mature if you can only be sure of three frost-free months.

Preparing the Garden

Taking the time to properly prepare your garden beds will save you time and effort throughout summer. Starting out with as few weeds as possible and with well-prepared soil that has had organic material added will give your edibles a good start. For container gardens, use potting soil because regular garden soil loses its structure when used in pots, quickly compacting into a solid mass that drains poorly.

Loosen the soil with a large garden fork and remove the weeds. Avoid working the soil when it is very wet or very dry because you will damage the soil structure by breaking down the pockets that hold air and water. Add good quality compost and work it into the soil with a spade, fork or rototiller. To determine how much compost you need, measure the area of your garden and then calculate how much compost you would need to cover it with 5–10 cm (2–4") of compost.

Organic matter is a small but important component of soil. It increases the water-holding and nutrient-holding capacity of sandy soil and binds together the large particles. In a clay soil, organic matter will increase the water-absorbing

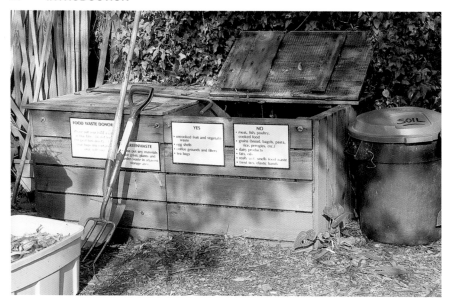

and draining potential by opening up spaces between the tiny particles. Common organic additives for your soil include grass clippings, shredded leaves, peat moss, chopped straw and well-rotted manure.

Composting

Any organic matter you add will be of greater benefit to your soil if it has been composted first. In natural environments, compost is created when leaves, plant bits and other debris are broken down on the soil surface. This process will also take place in your garden beds if you work fresh organic matter into the soil. However, microorganisms that break down organic matter use the same nutrients as your plants. The tougher the organic matter, the more nutrients in the soil will be used trying to break the matter down, thus robbing your plants of vital nutrients, particularly nitrogen. Also, fresh organic matter and garden debris might encourage or introduce pests and diseases in your garden.

A compost pile or bin, which can be built or purchased, creates a controlled environment where organic matter can be fully broken down before being introduced to your garden. Good composting methods also reduce the possibility of spreading pests and disease.

Creating compost is a simple process. Vegetable kitchen scraps, grass clippings and autumn leaves will slowly break down if left in a pile. You can speed up the process by following a few simple guidelines:

• Put both dry and fresh materials into your compost, with a larger proportion of dry matter such as chopped straw, shredded leaves or sawdust. Fresh green matter, such as vegetable scraps, grass clippings or pulled weeds, breaks down quickly and produces nitrogen, which feeds the decomposer organisms while they break down the tougher dry matter.

• Layer the green matter with the dry matter and mix in small amounts of soil from your garden or previously finished compost—it will introduce beneficial microorganisms. If the pile seems

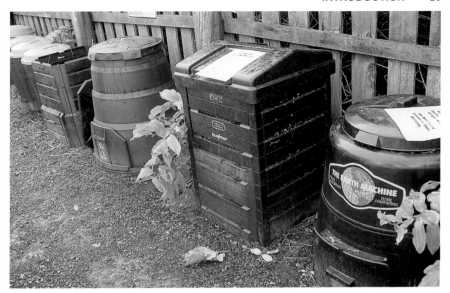

very dry, sprinkle on some water—the compost should be moist but not soaking wet, like a wrung-out sponge.

- Every week or two, turn the pile over or poke holes into it. Aerating the material will speed up decomposition. A compost pile that is kept aerated can generate a lot of heat. Temperatures can reach up to 70° C (160° F), or more. Such high temperatures destroy weed seeds and kill many damaging organisms. Most beneficial organisms are not killed until the temperature rises higher than 70° C (160° F). To monitor the temperature of the compost near the middle of the pile, you will need a thermometer attached to a long probe, similar to a large meat thermometer. Turning your compost when the temperature reaches 70° C (160° F) will stimulate the process to heat up again, but will prevent the temperatures from becoming high enough to kill the beneficial organisms.

- Don't put diseased or pest-ridden materials into your compost pile. If the damaging organisms are not destroyed,

they could spread throughout your garden.

- When you can no longer recognize the matter that you put into the compost bin, and the temperature no longer rises upon turning, your compost is ready to be mixed into your garden beds. Getting to this point can take as little as one month and will leave you with organic material that is rich in nutrients and beneficial organisms.

Compost can also be purchased from most garden centres.

Selecting Edible Plants

Many gardeners consider the trip to the local garden centre to pick out plants an important rite of spring, and many garden centres offer a few basic vegetable plants. Other gardeners find it rewarding to start their own plants from seed. Both methods have benefits, and you might want to use a combination of the two. Purchasing plants provides you with plants that are well grown, which is useful if you don't have the room or the facilities to start seeds. Some seeds require specific conditions that are difficult to achieve in a house, or they have erratic germination rates, which makes starting them yourself impractical. However, starting from seed offers you a far greater selection of species and varieties because seed catalogues often list many more plants than are offered at garden centres. Starting from seed is discussed starting on p. 25.

When browsing through a catalogue, you may find references to hybrid and heirloom seeds. Hybrids are generally newer selections of plants. They have been bred for specific traits such as flavour, size, disease resistance or improved storability. Often developed for market growers and food exporters, hybrids usually have traits that make them suitable for packing and transporting long distances without spoiling. Many have also become favourites amongst home gardeners since their introduction. These rarely come true to type from collected seed.

Heirloom refers to plant selections that have been in cultivation for generations. Many gardeners like the connection with history, knowing that their grandparents grew the same plant. Some of the most intriguing vegetable selections are heirlooms, and many advocates claim the vegetables to be among the tastiest and most pest and disease resistant. Seeds can be collected from the plants, and offspring will be true to type.

Purchased plants are grown in a variety of containers. Some are sold in individual pots, some in divided cell-packs and others in undivided trays. Each type has advantages and disadvantages.

Plants in individual pots are usually well established and generally have plenty of space for root growth. These plants have probably been seeded in flat trays and then transplanted into individual pots once they developed a few leaves. The cost of labour, pots and soil can make this option more expensive.

Plants grown in cell-packs are often inexpensive and hold several plants, making them easy to transport. There is less damage to the roots of the plants when they are transplanted, but because each cell is quite small, it doesn't take too long for a plant to become root-bound.

Hybrid corn stays sweet when picked.

Plants grown in undivided trays have plenty of room for root growth and can be left in the trays for longer than other types of containers, but their roots tend to become entangled, making the plants difficult to separate.

Regardless of the type of container, you should check for roots emerging from the holes at the bottom of the cells, or gently remove the plant from the container to look at the roots. If there are too many roots, the plant is too mature for the container, especially if the roots are wrapped around the inside of the container in a thick web. Such plants are slow to establish once they are transplanted into the garden.

The plants should be compact and have good colour. Healthy leaves look

Lemon cucumber is a tasty heirloom.

Unhealthy plant (above left), healthy plant (right)

firm and vibrant. Unhealthy leaves may be wilted, chewed or discoloured. Tall, leggy plants have likely been deprived of light. Sickly plants may not survive being transplanted and may spread pests or diseases.

Once you get your plants home, water them if they are dry. Plants growing in small containers may require water more than once a day. Begin to harden off the plants so they can be transplanted into the garden as soon as possible. Your plants are probably accustomed to growing in the sheltered environment of a greenhouse, and they will need to become accustomed to the climate outdoors. Placing them outdoors in a lightly shaded spot each day and bringing them into a sheltered porch, garage or house each night for about a week will acclimatize them to your garden.

Rootbound plant (centre), cutting roots before planting (bottom)

Nasturtium seeds (left), sunflower seeds (right)

Starting Edibles from Seed

Dozens of catalogues from different growers offer edible plants that you can start from seed. Many gardeners spend their chilly winter evenings poring through seed catalogues and planning their spring and summer gardens. Other places to find seeds include the Internet, local garden centres and seed exchange groups.

Starting your own plants can save you money, particularly if you need a lot of plants. The basic equipment is not expensive, and most seeds can be started in a sunny window. However, one or two trays don't take up too much room, but you may run out of room if you start more than that. That is why many gardeners start a few specialty plants themselves but buy most plants from a garden centre.

Each plant in this book has specific information on starting it from seed, if any is required, but a few basic steps can be followed for all seeds. The easiest way for the home gardener to start seeds is in cell-packs in trays with plastic dome covers. The cell-packs keep roots separated, and the tray and dome keep moisture in.

Seeds can also be started in pots, peat pots or peat pellets. The advantage to starting in peat pots or pellets is that you will not disturb the roots when you transplant.

Why start early? Many edible plants need a long period of warm weather to mature. If the seed is sown directly into the garden after the risk of frost has passed, there might not be enough time for the plants to mature before the first autumn frost ends the season.

Use a growing mix (soil mix) that is intended for seedlings. These mixes are very fine, usually made from peat moss, vermiculite and perlite. The mix will have good water-holding capacity and will have been sterilized to prevent pests and diseases from attacking your seedlings. One problem that can be caused by soil-borne fungi is damping off. The affected seedling will appear to have been pinched at soil level. The pinched area blackens and the seedling topples over and dies. Using sterile soil mix, keeping soil evenly moist and maintaining good air circulation will prevent plants from damping off.

Fill your pots or seed trays with the soil mix and firm it down slightly. Soil that is too firmly packed will not drain well. Wet the soil before planting your seeds to prevent them from getting washed around. Large seeds can be planted one or two to a cell, but place smaller seeds in a folded piece of paper and sprinkle them evenly over the soil surface. Very tiny seeds can be mixed

with fine sand and then sprinkled on the soil surface.

Small seeds do not need to be covered with any more soil, but medium-sized seeds can be lightly covered, and large

seeds can be poked into the soil. Some seeds need to be exposed to light to germinate; these should be left on the soil surface regardless of their size.

Additional light keeps plants healthy indoors.

Potting up gives seedlings room to grow.

Place pots or flats of seeds in plastic bags to retain humidity while the seeds are germinating. Many planting trays come with clear plastic covers that keep in the moisture. Remove the plastic once the seeds have germinated.

Water seeds and small seedlings gently with a fine spray from a hand-held mister—small seeds can easily be washed around if the spray is too strong. I recall working at a greenhouse where the seed trays containing the annual flower sweet alyssum were once watered a little too vigorously. Sweet alyssum was soon growing just about everywhere—with other plants, in the gravel on the floor and, oddly, in some of the flowerbeds outside. The lesson is "water gently."

Seeds provide all the energy and nutrients that young seedlings require. Small seedlings do not need to be fertilized until they have about four or five true leaves. When the first leaves that sprouted begin to shrivel, the plant has used up all its seed energy, and you can begin to use a fertilizer diluted to one-quarter.

If the seedlings get too big for their containers before you are ready to plant out, you may have to "up-pot" them to prevent them from becoming root-bound. Harden plants off by exposing them to outdoor conditions for longer every day for at least a week before planting them out.

Broccoli (top), cucumber (centre), watermelon (bottom)

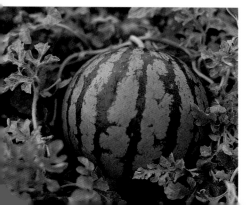

Edibles to Start Indoors
Artichoke
Basil
Broccoli and other *Brassica* spp.
Celery
Cucumber
Eggplant
Leek
Melon
Okra
Pepper
Squash
Tomato
Watermelon

Some seeds can be planted directly in the garden. The procedure is similar to that of starting seeds indoors. Begin with a well-prepared bed that has been smoothly raked. The small furrows left by the rake help hold moisture and prevent the seeds from being washed away. Sprinkle the seeds onto the soil and cover them lightly with peat moss or more soil. Larger seeds can be planted slightly deeper. Very tiny seeds should be mixed with sand for more even sowing. The soil should be kept moist to ensure even germination. Use a gentle spray to avoid washing the seeds around the bed because they inevitably pool into dense clumps. Cover your newly seeded bed with chicken wire, an old sheet or some thorny branches to discourage pets from digging.

Larger seeds are easy to space out well when you sow them. With smaller seeds, you may find that the new plants need to be thinned out to give adjacent plants room to grow properly. Pull out the weaker plants when groups look crowded. Some are edible and can be used as spring greens in a salad or steamed as a side dish.

Edibles for Direct Seeding
Amaranth
Beans
Beets
Carrots
Chard
Coriander
Corn
Lettuce
Nasturtium
Parsley
Peas
Quinoa
Radish
Sunflower

Beets

Lettuce

Quinoa

Peas

Growing Edibles

Once your plants have hardened off, it is time to plant them out. If your beds are already prepared, you are ready to start. The only tool you are likely to need is a trowel. Be sure you have set aside enough time to do the job. You don't want to have young plants out of their pots and not finish planting them. If they are left out in the sun, they can quickly dry out and die. To help avoid this problem, choose an overcast day for planting.

Planting

Plants are easier to remove from their containers if the soil is moist. Push on the bottom of the cell or pot with your thumb to ease the plants out. If the plants were growing in an undivided tray, you will have to gently untangle the roots. If the roots are very tangled, immerse them in water and wash some of the soil away. This should free the plants from one another. If you must handle the plant, hold it by a leaf to avoid crushing the stems. Remove and discard any damaged leaves or growth.

The rootball should contain a network of white plant roots. If the rootball is densely matted and twisted, break the tangles apart with your thumbs to encourage the roots to extend and grow outward. New root growth will start from the breaks, allowing the plant to spread outwards.

Plants started in peat pots and peat pellets can be planted pot and all. When planting peat pots into the garden, remove the top 4–6 cm (1½–2½") of pot. If any of the pot is sticking up out of the soil, it can wick moisture away from your plant.

Insert your trowel into the soil and pull it towards you, creating a wedge. Place your plant into the hole and firm the soil around it with your hands. Water gently but thoroughly. Until it is established, the plant will need regular watering.

Some of the plants in this book are sold in larger containers; others may be sold as bare roots or crowns, or in moistened peat moss, sphagnum moss or sawdust. A few are sold as bulbs, such as garlic and onion sets, which can be planted about three times as deep as the bulb is high.

Plants in larger containers can be planted as described above, except that they may require larger holes. In a prepared bed, dig a hole that will accommodate the rootball. Fill the hole in gradually, settling the soil with water as you go.

Plants that are sold without soil should be soaked in water for a few hours before planting as above, again being sure to accommodate the roots.

More detailed planting instructions are given, as needed, in the plant accounts.

Weeding

Controlling weed populations keeps the garden healthy and neat. Weeding may not be anyone's favourite task, but it is essential. Weeds compete with plants for light, nutrients and space,

and they can also harbour pests and disease.

Weeds can be pulled by hand or with a hoe. Shortly after a rainfall, when the soil is soft and damp, is the easiest time to pull them. A hoe scuffed quickly across the soil surface will uproot small weeds and sever larger ones from their

Mulch keeps weed at bay.

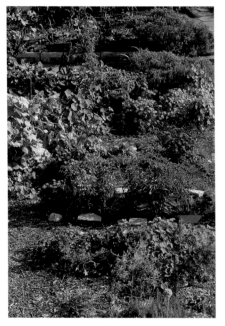

roots. Try to pull weeds out while they are still small. Once they are large enough to flower, many will quickly set seed; then you will have an entire new generation to worry about.

Mulching

A layer of mulch around your plants prevents light from reaching weed seeds, keeping them from germinating. Those that do germinate will be smothered or will be unable to reach the surface, exhausting their energy before getting a chance to grow.

Mulch also helps maintain consistent soil temperatures and ensures that moisture is retained effectively. In areas that receive heavy wind or rainfall, mulch can protect soil and prevent erosion. Mulching is effective in garden beds and planters.

Organic mulches such as compost, grass clippings or shredded leaves add nutrients to soil as they break down, thus improving the quality of the soil and, ultimately, the health of your plants.

Spread about 5–10 cm (2–4") of mulch over the soil after you have finished planting, or spread your mulch first and then make spaces to plant afterwards. Make sure the mulch is not piled thickly around the crowns and stems of your plants. Mulch that is too close to plants traps moisture, prevents air circulation and encourages fungal disease. Replenish your mulch as it breaks down over summer.

develop a deeper root system. In a dry spell, they will be adapted to seeking out water trapped deep in the ground. Use mulch to prevent water from evaporating out of the soil.

Be sure the water penetrates at least 10 cm (4") into the soil; this is approximately 2.5 cm (1") of applied water. To save time, money and water, you may wish to install an irrigation system, which applies the water exactly where it is needed, near the roots. Consult with your local garden centres or landscape professionals for more information.

Plants in hanging baskets and planters will probably need to be watered more frequently than plants in the ground—even twice daily during hot, sunny weather. The smaller the container, the more often the plants need watering.

Watering

Water thoroughly but infrequently. Plants given a light sprinkle of water every day develop roots that stay close to the soil surface, making the plants vulnerable to heat and dry spells. Plants given a deep watering once a week

A soaker hose provides a deeply penetrating application of water with less evaporation and run-off than a sprinkler.

Soaker hose arranged on a raised bed.

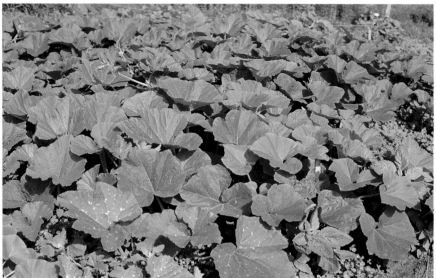

Squash are heavy feeders.

Fertilizing

We demand a lot of growth and production from many of our edible plants; annual ones in particular are expected to grow to maturity and provide us with a good crop of fruit or vegetables. They, in return, demand a lot of sun, nutrients and water. Mixing plenty of compost into the soil is a good start, but fertilizing regularly can make a big difference when it comes time to harvest your crop.

Whenever possible, use organic fertilizers because they are generally less concentrated and less likely to burn the roots of your plants. Organic fertilizers generally improve the soil as they feed your plants. Your local garden centre should carry organic fertilizers. Follow the directions carefully—using too much fertilizer can kill your plants by burning their roots and may upset the microbial balance of your soil, allowing pathogens to move in or dominate.

Fertilizer comes in many forms. Liquids or water-soluble powders are easiest to use when watering. Slow-release pellets or granules are mixed into the garden or potting soil or are sprinkled around the plant and left to work over summer.

Organic amendments (left to right): moisture-holding granules, earthworm castings, glacial dust, mycorrhizae, bat guano, compost, bone meal and coir fibre.

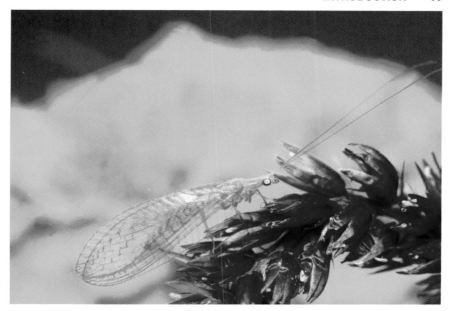

Problems & Pests

New edible plants are planted each spring and may be a different species each year. These factors make it difficult for pests and diseases to find their preferred host plants and establish a population. However, because many edibles are closely related, any problems that set in over summer are likely to attack all the plants in the same family.

For many years, pest control meant spraying or dusting with the goal to eliminate every pest in the landscape. A more moderate approach advocated today is IPM (Integrated Pest Management or Integrated Plant Management). The goal of IPM is to reduce pest problems so only negligible damage is done. Of course, you must determine what degree of damage is acceptable to you. Consider whether a pest's damage is localized or covers the entire plant. Will the damage kill the plant or is it only affecting the outward appearance?

Beneficial bugs: lacewing (top), ladybug (centre), ladybug larvae (below)

Coriander flowers attract beneficial insects.

Are there methods of controlling the pest without chemicals?

A good IPM program includes learning about your plants and the conditions they need for healthy growth, which pests might affect your plants, where and when to look for those pests and how to control them. Keep records of pest damage because your observations can reveal patterns useful in spotting recurring problems and in planning your maintenance regime.

There are four steps in effective and responsible pest management. Cultural controls are the most important and are the first response when problems arise.

Physical controls should be attempted next, followed by biological controls. Resort to chemical controls only when the first three possibilities have been exhausted.

Cultural controls are the gardening techniques you use in the day-to-day care of your garden. Keeping your plants as healthy as possible is the best defence against pests. Growing plants in the conditions they prefer and keeping your soil healthy by adding plenty of organic matter are just two of the cultural controls you can use to keep pests manageable. Choose resistant varieties of plants that are not prone to problems.

Space the plants so that they have good air circulation around them and are not stressed by competing for light, nutrients and space. Take plants that are decimated by the same pests every year out of the landscape. Remove diseased foliage and branches, and burn it or take it to a permitted dumpsite. Prevent the spread of disease by keeping gardening tools clean and by tidying up fallen leaves and dead plant matter at the end of every growing season.

Physical controls are generally used to combat insect problems: picking insects off plants by hand, barriers that stop insects from getting to the plant, and traps that catch or confuse insects. Physical control of disease often necessitates removing the infected plant part or parts to prevent the spread of the problem.

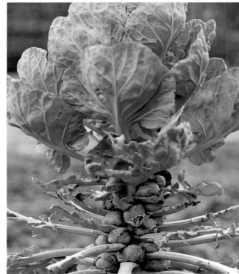

Brussel sprouts (above), horseradish (below)

Biological controls use predators that prey on pests. Animals such as birds, snakes, frogs, spiders, lady beetles and certain bacteria can play an important role in keeping pest populations manageable. Encourage these creatures to take up permanent residence in your garden. A birdbath and birdfeeder will encourage birds to enjoy your yard and feed on a wide variety of insect pests. Many beneficial insects are probably already living in your landscape, and you can encourage them to stay by planting appropriate food sources. Many beneficial insects eat nectar from flowers such as coriander and perennial yarrow.

Chemical controls should rarely be necessary, but if you must use them, there are some "organic" options available. Organic sprays are no less dangerous than chemical ones, but they break down into harmless compounds. The main drawback to using any chemicals

One of the most effective methods of reducing disease problems in an edible garden is crop rotation—don't put the same plant, or even one from the same family, in the same location two years in a row. By changing the crop from year to year, you can prevent problems from setting in annually. It is best to wait two years before planting any member of a family in the same location (the Brassica family, for example, includes broccoli, Brussels sprouts, cabbage, cauliflower, collards, horseradish, kale, kohlrabi, mustard, oriental cabbage, radish, rutabaga and turnip).

is that they may also kill the beneficial insects you have been trying to attract to your garden. Organic chemicals are available at most garden centres.

Follow the manufacturer's instructions carefully. A large amount of pesticide is not going to be any more effective in controlling pests than the recommended amount. Note that if a particular pest is not listed on the package, that product will not control the pest. Proper and early identification of pests is vital to finding a quick solution.

Whereas cultural, physical, biological and chemical controls are all possible defences against insects, diseases can only be controlled culturally. It is most often weakened plants that succumb to diseases. Healthy plants can often fight off illness, though some diseases can infect plants regardless of their level of health. Prevention is often the only hope; once a plant has been infected, it should probably be destroyed to prevent the disease from spreading.

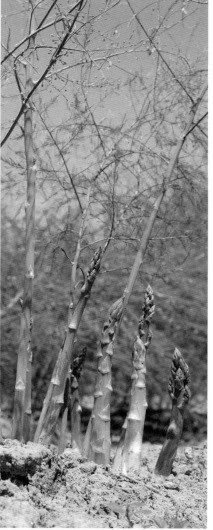

Insect damage disfigures Asparagus spears (left), healthy spears (right) are more appetizing.

Aphids

Beetles

Pests and Diseases

Anthracnose

Fungus. Yellow or brown spots on leaves; sunken lesions and blisters on stems; can kill plant.

What to Do: choose resistant varieties and cultivars; keep soil well drained; thin out stems to improve air circulation; avoid handling wet foliage; remove and destroy infected plant parts; clean up and destroy debris from infected plants at end of growing season.

Aphids

Tiny, pear-shaped, green, black, brown, red or grey insects; can be winged or wingless; e.g., woolly adelgids. Cluster along stems, on buds and on leaves; suck sap from plant; cause distorted or stunted growth; sticky honeydew forms on plant surfaces and encourages sooty mould growth.

What to Do: squish small colonies by hand; dislodge with brisk water spray; encourage predatory insects and birds that feed on aphids; spray serious infestations with insecticidal soap or neem oil according to package directions.

Aster Yellows

see Viruses

Beetles

Many types and sizes; usually rounded in shape with hard, shell-like outer wings covering membranous inner wings. Some are beneficial, e.g., ladybird beetles ("ladybugs"); others, e.g., Japanese beetles, leaf skeletonizers and weevils, eat plants. Larvae: see Borers, Grubs. Leave wide range of chewing damage: make small or large holes in or around margins of leaves; consume entire leaves or areas between leaf veins ("skeletonize"); may also chew holes in flowers. Some bark beetle species carry deadly plant diseases.

What to Do: pick beetles off at night and drop them into an old coffee can half filled with soapy water (soap prevents them from floating and climbing out).

Borer damage on squash

Mealybugs (see p. 44)

Blight

Fungal diseases. Many types; e.g., leaf blight, needle blight, snow blight. Leaves, stems and flowers blacken, rot and die.

What to Do: thin stems to improve air circulation; keep mulch away from base of plants; remove debris from garden at end of growing season; remove and destroy infected plant parts.

Borers

Larvae of some moths, wasps, beetles. Worm-like; vary in size and get bigger as they bore through plants; among the most damaging plant pests. Burrow into plant stems, branches, leaves and/or roots; destroy vascular tissue (plant veins and arteries) and structural strength; weaken stems to cause breakage; leaves will wilt; may see tunnels in leaves, stems or roots; rhizomes may be hollowed out entirely or in part.

What to Do: may be able to squish borers within leaves; remove and destroy bored parts; may need to dig up and destroy infected roots and rhizomes.

Bugs (True Bugs)

Small green, brown, black or brightly coloured and patterned insects, up to 1.3 cm (1/2") long. Many are beneficial; a few pests, such as lace bugs, pierce plants to suck out sap; toxins may be injected that deform plants; sunken areas remain where pierced; leaves rip

Lygus bug on cosmos flower

as they grow; leaves, buds and new growth may be dwarfed and deformed.

What to Do: remove debris and weeds from around plants in autumn to destroy overwintering sites. Spray plants with insecticidal soap or neem oil according to package directions.

Case Bearers
   see Caterpillars

Caterpillars
   Larvae of butterflies, moths, sawflies; include bagworms, budworms, case bearers, cutworms, leaf rollers, leaf tiers, loopers. Chew foliage and buds; can completely defoliate a plant if infestation is severe.

What to Do: removal from plant is best control; use high-pressure water and soap or pick caterpillars off small plants by hand. Control biologically using the naturally occurring soil bacterium *Bacillus thuringiensis* var. *kurstaki* or *B.t.k.* (commercially available), which breaks down the gut lining of caterpillars.

Caterpillar on roses

Spittlebugs are unsightly but rarely cause damage.

Cutworms

See Caterpillars

Deer

Can decimate crops, woodlands and gardens; can kill saplings by rubbing their antlers on the trees, girdling the bark or snapping the trees in two; host ticks that carry Lyme disease and Rocky Mountain spotted fever.

Deer-chewed cedars.

What to Do: many deterrents work for a while: encircle immature shrubs with tall upright sticks; place dangling soap bars around the garden; use noise-making devices or water spritzers to startle deer; mount flashy aluminium or moving devices throughout the garden.

Galls

Unusual swellings of plant tissues that may be caused by insects or diseases. Can affect leaves, buds, stems, flowers, fruit; often a specific gall affects a single genus or species.

What to Do: cut galls out of plant and destroy them. Galls caused by insects usually contain the insect's eggs and juvenile stages; prevent such galls by controlling the insect before it lays eggs; otherwise try to remove and destroy infected tissue before young insects emerge. Insect galls are generally more unsightly than damaging to plant; galls caused by diseases often require destruction of plant. Don't place other plants susceptible to same disease in that location.

Leaf miners

Grey Mould
See Blight

Grubs
Larvae of different beetles; white or grey body; head may be white, grey, brown or reddish; usually curled in C-shape; commonly found below soil level. Problematic in lawns; may feed on roots of perennials; plant wilts despite regular watering; may pull easily out of ground in severe cases.

What to Do: toss grubs onto a stone path, driveway, road or patio for birds to devour; apply parasitic nematodes or milky spore to infested soil (ask at your local garden centre).

Leafhoppers & Treehoppers
Small, wedge-shaped insects; can be green, brown, grey or multi-coloured; jump around frantically when disturbed. Suck juice from plant leaves; cause distorted growth; carry diseases such as aster yellows.

What to Do: encourage predators by planting nectar-producing species such as coriander. Wash insects off with strong spray of water; spray with insecticidal soap or neem oil according to package directions.

Leaf Miners
Tiny, stubby larvae of some butterflies and moths; may be yellow or green. Tunnel within leaves leaving winding trails; tunnelled areas lighter in colour than rest of leaf; unsightly rather than major health risk to plant.

What to Do: remove debris from area in autumn to destroy overwintering sites; attract parasitic wasps with nectar plants such as yarrow or coriander; remove and destroy infected foliage; can sometimes squish larvae by hand within leaf.

Leaf Rollers
see Caterpillars

Leaf Skeletonizers
see Beetles

Leaf Spot

Two common types: one caused by bacteria and the other by fungi. *Bacterial:* small brown or purple spots grow to encompass entire leaves; leaves may drop. *Fungal:* black, brown or yellow spots; leaves wither; e.g., scab, tar spot.

What to Do: *Bacterial:* infection more severe; must remove entire plant. *Fungal:* remove and destroy infected plant parts; sterilize removal tools; avoid wetting foliage or touching wet foliage; remove and destroy debris at end of growing season.

Cabbage root maggots on radishes

Maggots

Larvae of several species of flies (cabbage root maggots, carrot rust flies). Small, white or grey, worm-like. Tunnel into roots of a variety of plants, including many root vegetables. Stunts plants and disfigures roots; serious infestations can kill plants.

What to Do: Use floating row covers to prevent flies from laying eggs near roots. Apply parasitic nematodes to soil around plants. Use an early crop of radishes as a trap crop. Pull them up and destroy them as soon as they become infested with maggots.

Mealybugs

Tiny crawling insects related to aphids; appear to be covered with white fuzz or flour. Sucking damage stunts and stresses plant; excrete honeydew that promotes growth of sooty mould.

What to Do: remove by hand from smaller plants; wash plant with soap and water or wipe with alcohol-soaked swabs; remove heavily infested leaves; encourage or introduce natural predators such as mealybug destroyer beetle and parasitic wasps; spray with insecticidal soap. Larvae of mealybug destroyer beetles look like very large mealybugs.

Mice

Burrow under mulch in winter, chewing plant roots, bark, tulip bulbs and many other underground goodies; even plants or roots stored in cool porches, garages or sheds are fair game.

What to Do: fine wire mesh can prevent mice from getting at your plants in winter, though they are quite ingenious and may find their way through or around any barrier you erect; bulbs and lifted roots can be rolled in talcum powder, garlic powder or bulb protectant spray before storing or planting. Get a cat, or borrow your neighbour's, if you must.

Mildew

Two types, both caused by fungus, but with slightly different symptoms. *Downy mildew:* yellow spots on upper sides of leaves and downy fuzz on undersides; fuzz may be yellow, white or grey. *Powdery mildew:* white or grey powdery coating on leaf surfaces that doesn't brush off.

What to Do: choose resistant cultivars; space plants well; thin stems to encourage air circulation; tidy any debris in autumn; remove and destroy infected parts.

Mites

Tiny, red, yellow or green, eight-legged relatives of spiders; e.g., bud mites, spider mites, spruce mites; almost invisible to naked eye; do not eat insects, but may spin webs; usually found on undersides of plant leaves; may see fine webbing on leaves and stems or mites moving on leaf undersides. Suck juice out of leaves; leaves become discoloured and speckled, then turn brown and shrivel up.

What to Do: wash off with strong spray of water daily until all signs of infestation are gone; predatory mites are available through garden centres; spray plants with insecticidal soap.

Moles and Gophers

Burrow under the soil, tunnelling throughout your property in search of insects, grubs and earthworms; tunnels can create runways for voles that will eat your plants from below ground.

What to Do: castor oil (the primary ingredient in most repellents made to thwart moles and gophers) spilled down the mole's runway is effective and is

Powdery mildew on Black-Eyed Susan

available in granulated pellet form, too; noisemakers and predator urine are also useful; humane trapping is effective, as is having a cat or dog.

Mosaic

see Viruses

Nematodes

Tiny worms that give plants disease symptoms; one type infects foliage and stems; the other infects roots. *Foliar:* leaves have yellow spots that turn brown; leaves shrivel and wither; problem starts on lowest leaves and works up plant. *Root-knot:* plant is stunted and may wilt; yellow spots on leaves; roots have tiny bumps or knots.

What to Do: mulch soil; add organic matter; clean up debris in autumn; don't touch wet foliage of infected plants; can add parasitic nematodes to soil; remove infected plants in extreme cases.

Rabbits

Can eat as much of your garden as deer and munch on the bark of trees and shrubs.

What to Do: deterrents that work for deer usually keep rabbits away, as will humane trapping; having a cat or dog patrol your garden may also be effective.

Rot

Several different fungi that affect different parts of plant, sometimes even killing it. *Crown rot:* affects base of plant, causing stems to blacken and fall over and leaves to yellow and wilt. *Root rot:* leaves turn yellow and plant wilts; digging up plant shows roots rotted away. *White rot:* a "watery decay fungus" that affects any part of plant; cell walls appear to break down, releasing fluids.

What to Do: keep soil well drained; don't damage plant if you are digging around it; keep mulches away from plant base; destroy infected plant if whole plant is affected.

Raccoons

Are especially fond of fruit and some vegetables; can carry rabies and canine distemper; also eat grubs, insects and mice, so can sometimes be helpful to gardeners.

What to Do: don't allow access to garbage or pet food; humane traps and relocation are best solutions; call your local SPCA or Humane Society to relocate individuals.

Rust

Fungi; pale spots on upper leaf surfaces; orange, fuzzy or dusty spots on leaf undersides; e.g., blister rust, hollyhock rust.

What to Do: choose rust-resistant varieties and cultivars; avoid handling wet leaves; provide plant with good air circulation; clear up garden debris at end of season; remove and destroy infected plant parts.

Scab

see Leaf Spot

Scale Insects

Tiny, shelled insects that suck sap, weakening and possibly killing plant or making it vulnerable to other problems; once female scale insect has pierced plant with mouthpart, it is there for life; juvenile scale insects are called crawlers.

What to Do: wipe bugs off with alcohol-soaked swabs; spray plant with water to dislodge crawlers; prune out heavily infested branches; encourage natural predators and parasites; spray dormant oil in spring before bud break.

Slugs & Snails

Slugs lack shells; snails have a spiral shell; both have slimy, smooth skin; can be up to 20 cm (8") long but are often much smaller; grey, green, black, beige, yellow or spotted. Leave large ragged hole in leaves and silvery slime trails on and around plants.

What to Do: attach strips of copper to wood around raised beds or smaller boards inserted around susceptible groups of plants (slugs and snails get shocked if they touch copper surfaces); pick off by hand in the evening and squish or drop in a can of soapy water; spread wood ash or diatomaceous earth (available in garden centres) around plants (it pierces their soft bodies and causes them to dehydrate); slug baits containing iron phosphate are not harmful to humans or animals and control slugs very well; if slugs damaged garden last season, begin controls as soon as new green shoots appear in spring.

Sooty Mould

Fungus; thin black film forms on leaf surfaces and reduces amount of light getting to leaf surfaces.

Snails (above) and slugs (centre) can cause a lot of chewing damage to plants (below).

What to Do: Wipe mould off leaf surfaces; control aphids, mealybugs, whiteflies (honeydew left on leaves encourages mould).

Squirrels

Unearth and eat bulbs and corms, as well as flowers, fruits and vegetables; chew on sugar maples and hone their other teeth on almost everything else; raid birdfeeders and often eat the feeder itself; bury their food for later consumption, which can result in seeds germinating and plants springing up where you never wanted them.

Sticky pheremone traps are useful for monitoring insect populations.

What to Do: cut heavy metal screening (hardware cloth) to fit around the plant stem; caging entire plants is effective if you don't mind your garden looking like a zoo; removing enticing food supplies is effective, but often impractical; trapping and moving is one option but usually results in other squirrels moving in to take their place.

Tar Spot
see Leaf Spot

Thrips
Tiny, slender, yellow, black or brown insects; narrow, fringed wings; difficult to see but may be visible if you disturb them by blowing gently on an infested

flower. Suck juice out of plant cells, particularly in flowers and buds, causing mottled petals and leaves, dying buds, distorted and stunted growth.

What to Do: Remove and destroy infected plant parts; encourage native predatory insects with nectar plants like yarrow or coriander; spray severe infestations with insecticidal soap or neem oil according to package directions.

Viruses
Include aster yellows, mosaic virus, ringspot virus. Plant may be stunted and leaves and flowers distorted, streaked or discoloured.

What to Do: Viral diseases in plants cannot be treated. Control disease-spreading insects, such as aphids, leafhoppers and whiteflies; destroy infected plants.

Voles
Mouse-like creatures that damage plants at or just beneath the soil surface; mostly herbivorous, feeding on a variety of grasses, vegetables, herbaceous plants, bulbs (lilies are a favourite) and tubers; also eat bark and roots of trees, usually in autumn or winter, and store seeds and other plant matter in underground chambers.

What to Do: Wire fences at least 30 cm (12") high with a mesh size of 1 cm (½") or less and buried 15–20 cm (6–8") deep can help exclude voles from gardens. These fences can either stand alone or be attached to the bottom of an existing fence. A weed-free barrier on the outside of the fence will increase its effectiveness. Burrow fumigants do not effectively control voles because the vole's burrow system is shallow and has many open holes. Electromagnetic or ultrasonic devices and flooding are also ineffective. When vole populations are not numerous or concentrated in a small area, trapping may be effective. Use enough traps to control the population: for a small garden, use at least 12 traps, and for larger areas 50 or more may be needed. Again, a dog or cat is a deterrent. Do not use poisonous repellents or baits if your pets or children romp around the garden.

Weevils
see Beetles

Whiteflies
Tiny, white, moth-like, flying insects that flutter up into the air when plant is disturbed; live on undersides of plant leaves. Suck juice out of leaves, causing yellowed leaves and weakened plants; leave behind sticky honeydew on leaves, encouraging sooty mould growth.

What to Do: Destroy weeds where insects may live; attract native predatory beetles and parasitic wasps with nectar plants like yarrow or coriander; spray severe cases with insecticidal soap; can make a sticky flypaper-like trap by mounting a tin can on a stake, wrapping can with yellow paper and covering it with clear plastic bag smeared with petroleum jelly (replace bag when it's covered in flies).

Wilt
If watering doesn't help wilted plants, one of two wilt fungi may be to blame. *Fusarium wilt:* plant wilts; leaves turn yellow then die; symptoms generally appear first on one part of plant before spreading to other parts. *Verticillium wilt:* plant wilts; leaves curl up at edges; leaves turn yellow then drop off; plant may die.

What to Do: Both wilts are difficult to control; choose resistant plant varieties and cultivars; clean up debris at end

of growing season; destroy infected plants; solarize (sterilize) soil before replanting (may help if entire bed of plants lost to these fungi)—contact local garden centre for assistance.

Woolly Adelgids
see Aphids

Worms
see Caterpillars, Nematodes

Homemade Insecticidal Soap
5 ml (1 tsp) mild dish detergent or pure soap (biodegradable options are available)
1 litre (4 cups) water
Mix in a clean spray bottle and spray the surfaces of your plants. Rinse well within an hour to avoid foliage discoloration.

About this Guide

The plants featured here are organized alphabetically by their most common familiar names. Additional common names appear as well. This system enables you to find a plant easily if you are familiar with only the common name. The scientific or botanical name is always listed after the common name. I encourage you to learn these botanical names. Several plants may share the same common name, and they vary from region to region. Only the specific botanical name identifies the specific plant anywhere in the world.

Clearly indicated within each entry are the plant's height and spread ranges, outstanding features and hardiness zone(s), if applicable. Each entry gives clear instructions for planting and growing the plants, and recommends many favourite selections. If height and spread ranges or hardiness zones are not given for every recommended plant, assume these ranges are the same as those provided in the Features section. Your local garden centre will have any additional information about the plant and will help you make your plant selections.

Finally, the Pests and Diseases section of the introduction deals with issues that afflict your garden plants from time to time.

Amaranth

Amaranthus

Features: bushy upright annual; red, purple, burgundy, gold or green plume-like flower clusters; edible young growth and seeds **Height:** 1.2–2.7 m (4–9')
Spread: 30–90 cm (11–36")

Amaranth provides one of the most complete sources of protein available in a grain. This drought-resistant plant is prolific, producing up to 10,000 seeds in a single flowerhead.

Combine amaranth with sunflowers for an impressive late season display. The seedheads of both will be ready for harvesting at about the same time.

A. hypochondriacus (above)

Starting

Amaranth sprouts quickly when sown directly in the garden. Scatter seeds or plant in rows once all danger of frost has passed and the soil has warmed—mid-May to early June for most Canadian gardens.

Growing

Amaranth grows best in **full sun**. It adapts to most soil conditions, but it prefers a **fertile** soil. Spread a layer of compost on the soil before you plant to keep weeds down and to improve the soil. Although it is drought tolerant, this plant grows best if the soil is kept fairly moist while it germinates.

Harvesting

The seeds usually ripen and fall about the time of the first autumn frost. Several harvesting methods can be used. Over a drop cloth, large bowl or bucket, shake or rub the seedheads between your hands—wear gloves, because the seedheads can be quite coarse. The seeds and plant bits are easy to separate because the plant bits are lighter and rise to the surface if you run your hands through the collected seeds and carefully blow a fan over them. The seeds are quite light, too, so the breeze should not be too strong. Leave the seeds to dry in a warm place before storing them in an airtight container.

Tips

This plant is very tall and makes a good screen plant. It resembles giant celosia when in bloom and is indeed related to that popular annual. The flowers can be used in fresh or dried arrangements, but cutting the flowers will reduce your yield.

Young leaves can be steamed and eaten like spinach. The grains can be added to soups and stews, cooked as a hot cereal or side dish, or ground into flour and used in pancakes, muffins and breads. They can even be popped, like corn, for snacking.

Recommended

A. hypochondriacus (amaranth, grain amaranth) is a tall annual plant that bears large plume-like clusters of red, purple, gold or green flowers. It grows 1.2–2.7 m (4–9') tall and spreads up to 90 cm (3'). Several cultivars are available, including **'Burgundy,'** with purple-red leaves and large burgundy plumes; **'Golden Giant,'** with bright yellow stems and flowers that mature to deep gold; and **'Mercado,'** with dense, less plume-like, bright green flowerheads.

Problems and Pests

Young plants look very similar to red-rooted pigweed, making weeding challenging. If red-rooted pigweed is common in your garden, start your amaranth plants in peat pots, then transplant them directly into the garden to make weed identification easier.

Artichoke

Globe Artichoke

Cynara

Features: bushy tender perennial; edible flower buds; spiny foliage; purple thistle-like flowers **Height:** 60 cm–2 m (2–7') **Spread:** 60 cm–1.2 m (2–4')

Artichokes are one of those vegetables that require a little extra effort to grow successfully in Canada. These members of the thistle family are tender perennials native to the Mediterranean. With a thick mulch, they may survive winter in southern Ontario and on the West Coast. For the rest of us, choosing a quick-maturing cultivar and starting very early is the best way to enjoy homegrown artichokes.

Starting

Start seed indoors about eight weeks before the last frost date or up to 12 weeks before the last frost date if you have a very bright location or supplemental lighting available. Plant seeds into the largest size of peat pots. These plants don't like to have their roots disturbed, and you want to encourage them to grow as much as possible before they are planted into the garden. You can also purchase started plants, but you may have to shop early because their availability is low and often only specialty nurseries carry them.

Plant artichokes outdoors after the last frost date. These are very wide-spreading plants, so plant them at least 60 cm (2') apart the first year and eventually up to 1.2 m (4') apart, if you overwinter them successfully.

Growing

Artichokes grow best in **full sun,** though they appreciate some afternoon shade in hotter locations. The soil should be **fertile, humus rich, moist** and **well drained**. Mix compost into the soil in spring, and use a layer of compost on the soil as a mulch. These plants like plenty of water but don't like a soggy soil. Replenish the compost mulch in mid-summer, if needed. If the buds are just beginning to form, and heavy frost is expected, you can cover the plants with sheets at night to extend the growing season.

On the West Coast, in southern Ontario and even in warmer parts of the Maritimes, artichokes may survive winter. If they are planted near a house foundation or other place where the soil doesn't freeze completely, plants can be protected with a thick layer of straw. A layer 30–45 cm (12–18") deep will help keep the soil temperatures more consistent.

In other parts of Canada, we can either treat these plants like annuals or dig up the roots once the leaves die back in autumn, clean off any soil and store them in slightly moistened peat or sphagnum moss in a cold, frost-free location for winter. Check them over winter, and if they are beginning to sprout, pot them and keep them in the brightest indoor location you can find until they can be planted outdoors again.

Harvesting

Artichokes produce one large flower bud on the central stalk and many smaller flower buds on the side shoots. The flower buds are rounded and made up of tightly packed scales. They are usually ready for harvest as the scales just begin to loosen. With luck and an early enough start, you should have a good crop the first year in autumn. If overwintered successfully, artichokes generally flower earlier in the season, in June or July.

Tips
With a sharp knife, cut the flower bud from the plant about 10–15 cm (4–6") below the bud's base.

Artichoke plants make dramatic additions to vegetable and ornamental gardens. The flowers are quite stunning and can be used in fresh flower arrangements if not eaten while in bud form. If you are going to try to overwinter artichokes in the ground, plant them in a place where the soil stays warmest in winter. This spot is often dry in summer, so mulch well to retain soil moisture.

Recommended
C. scolymus forms a large clump of deeply lobed, pointy-tipped, grey-green leaves. It grows 60 cm–2 m (2–7') tall and spreads 60 cm–1.2 m (2–4'). In autumn or sometimes summer, it bears large, scaled flower buds that open if not picked for eating. **'Green Globe'** is one of the most popular cultivars because it is tasty and is one of the quickest to mature and flower.

Problems and Pests
Rare problems with mould, root rot, slugs and aphids are possible.

Asparagus

Asparagus

Features: perennial; edible spring shoots; ferny growth; small white summer flowers; decorative red fruit **Height:** 60 cm–1.5 m (2–5') **Spread:** 60 cm–1.2 m (2–4')

The large, ferny growth that asparagus develops comes as quite a surprise to first-time growers who may have only seen tidy bunches of spears at the grocery store. Asparagus is a member of the lily family, and well-established plants can last a lifetime, producing tasty spears every spring.

Starting

Asparagus can be started from seed, or you can buy roots (also called crowns). A plant started from seed will be ready to start harvesting the third spring. A plant started from roots will be ready to begin harvesting the second spring.

Plant purchased roots into a well-prepared area. Work plenty of compost into the bed, then dig a trench or hole about 45 cm (18") deep. Lay the roots 45–60 cm (18–24") apart from each other or other plants. Cover the roots with 5–10 cm (2–4") of soil and, as they sprout up, gradually cover them with more soil until the trench or hole is filled. Water and mulch well.

Plant seeds indoors in flats or peat pots about 6–8 weeks before you will be planting them into the garden. Use larger pots if the seedlings get too big before the last frost date has passed and you can move them outside. The first year, you should plant the seedlings at the soil level they are at in their pots. Keep them well watered and mulch them with compost. The second summer, they can be planted as for roots, described above.

Asparagus is dioecious—male and female flowers are borne on separate plants. Male plants are reputed to produce the greatest number of spears.

A. officinalis 'Mary Washington' (above)

Growing

Asparagus grows well in **full sun** or **partial shade** with **protection** from the hot afternoon sun. The soil should be **fertile, humus rich, moist** and **well drained.** Apply a 10 cm (4") layer of compost in spring and late summer. Weed regularly, because this plant is most productive if it doesn't have a lot of competition from other plants.

Harvesting

As mentioned, asparagus spears that were started from roots are ready to be harvested two years after planting; spears started from seeds are ready in three years. Snap or cut the spears off at ground level for up to about four weeks in spring and early summer. When new spears are thinner than a pencil, you should stop harvesting and let the plants grow in. Add a new layer of compost to the soil when you have finished harvesting.

Tips
This hardy perennial plant is a welcome treat in spring and a beautiful addition to the back of a border.

Recommended
A. officinalis forms an airy mound of ferny growth. It grows 60 cm– 1.5 m (2–5') tall and spreads 60 cm– 1.2 m (2–4'). Small white summer flowers are followed by bright red berries, which can be collected for starting new plants. **'Jersey Giant,' 'Martha Washington,' 'Mary Washington'** and **'Guelph Millennium'** are all good cultivars that are readily available.

Problems and Pests
Rust can be a problem, so choose resistant cultivars.

A. officinalis 'Mary Washington' (above)

Asparagus has been a cultivated vegetable crop for over 2000 years.

Basil

Ocimum

Features: fragrant, decorative leaves; white or light purple flowers
Height: 30–60 cm (12–24")
Spread: 30–45 cm (12–18")

The sweet, fragrant leaves of basil add a delicious, licorice-like flavour to salads and tomato-based dishes.

O. basilicum (above)

Starting
Basil is easy to start from seed. Start seeds indoors about four weeks before the last frost date, or sow seed directly outdoors once the last frost date has passed and the soil has warmed up. Press seeds into the soil and sift a little more soil over them. Keep the soil moist. Generally seeds will germinate within a week.

Growing
Basil grows best in a **warm, sheltered** location in **full sun**. The soil should be **fertile, moist** and **well drained**. Pinch the tips regularly to encourage bushy growth. Mulch soil to retain water and keep weeds down.

Harvesting
Pluck leaves or pinch back stem tips as needed. Basil is tastiest if used fresh, but it can be dried or frozen for use in winter.

Tips
Although basil grows best in a warm spot outdoors, it can be grown successfully indoors in a pot by a bright window, providing you with fresh leaves all year.

Pinch off any flowering tips that form to encourage leaf production.

Recommended
O. basilicum is a bushy annual or short-lived perennial with bright green, fragrant leaves. It bears white or light purple flowers in mid- to late summer. There are many cultivars of basil, with varied leaf sizes, shapes, colours and flavours.

Problems and Pests
Fusarium wilt is probably the worst problem that afflicts basil.

Basil makes a great companion for tomatoes because they both require warm, moist growing conditions and are delicious when eaten together.

Bay Laurel
Laurus

Features: tender evergreen shrub; aromatic foliage
Height: 30 cm–1.2 m (1–4') **Spread:** 20–60 cm (8–24")

Bay leaves are commonly used in soups and
stews. The plants are easy to grow and are
attractive houseplants.

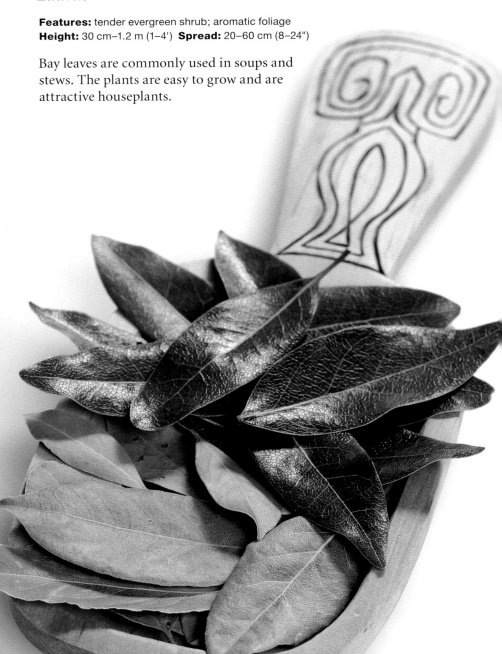

Starting

Bay laurel can be started from seed, but germination may take up to six months. Plant the seeds in warm soil and keep the environment warm and moist but not wet or the seeds will rot. It is simpler to purchase started plants, which are available from specialty growers and nurseries.

Growing

Bay laurel grows well in **full sun** or **partial shade**. A plant that will be moved indoors for winter should be grown in partial or light shade in summer. The soil should be **fertile, moist** and **well drained**. This plant is shallow-rooted and can dry out quickly in hot or windy weather. Mulch to reduce evaporation.

In winter, move bay laurel indoors and keep it in a cool but sunny room; continue to water it regularly, as needed.

Harvesting

It may take a couple of years before your bay laurel is leafy enough to be used on a regular basis. Pick fresh leaves as needed to use in cooking. Leaves can be dried and stored for later use, but this plant is evergreen, so you should be able to pick fresh leaves all year.

Tips

Bay laurel is best grown in containers in Canada, because the plants need to be brought indoors during freezing weather. It makes an attractive addition to patios, decks and on the steps of a staircase with other potted herbs, vegetables and flowers.

L. nobilis (above)

Recommended

L. nobilis is a bushy evergreen shrub. It grows up to 12 m (40') tall in the Mediterranean, where it is native. In containers it can be kept to a far more manageable size of 30 cm–1.2 m (1–4') in height and 20–60 cm (8–24") in spread. Plants rarely flower in Canada. **'Aureus'** is a cultivar with golden yellow foliage.

Problems and Pests

Rare problems with scale insects and mealybugs can occur, but these are usually easy enough to wash or rub off smaller plants. Powdery mildew can occur in poorly ventilated situations.

Beans

Phaseolus

Features: tender bushy or twining annual; attractive foliage; red, white or bicoloured flowers; edible pods or seeds **Height:** 30 cm–2.4 m (1–8') **Spread:** 30–45 cm (12–18")

This incredibly diverse group of legumes includes beans eaten as pods, as immature seeds or as mature, dry seeds. Plants can be low and bushy or tall and twining. Plants are often prolific and some are very attractive.

Starting

Beans are quite possibly one of the easiest plants to grow from seed. They are large and easy to handle, and they sprout quickly in warm, moist soil. Plant them directly in the garden after the last frost date has passed and the soil has warmed up. They can be planted 10–20 cm (4–8") apart.

Growing

Beans grow best in **full sun**, but they tolerate some light afternoon shade. The soil should be of **average fertility** and **well drained**. Bush beans are self-supporting, but climbing beans need a pole or trellis to grow up. The support structure should be in place at planting time so you can avoid disturbing the young plants or damaging their roots.

Bush beans can become less productive and look unattractive as summer wears on. Pull them up and plant something else in their place, or plant them with companions that mature more slowly to fill in the space left by the faded bean plants.

Harvesting

The most important thing to remember when harvesting beans is to do so only when the foliage is dry. Touching wet foliage or plants encourages the spread of disease.

Different types of beans should be picked at different stages in their development. Green, runner, wax or snap beans are picked once the pod is a good size but still young and tender. As they mature, they

Legumes, like beans, are known for being able to fix nitrogen from the air into the soil. They do this through a symbiotic relationship with bacteria, which attach to the roots as small nodules. The bacteria turn the nitrogen from the air into useable nitrogen for the plant; in return the plant feeds and supports the bacteria. The bacteria are present in most soils and are also available for purchase as a soil inoculant. Some bean seeds are also pre-treated with the bacteria.

P. vulgaris (above), *P. lunatus* (below)

become stringy, woody and dry. Beans that are eaten as immature seeds should be picked when the pods are full and the seeds are fleshy and moist.

Beans for drying are left to mature on the plant. Once the plant begins to die back and before the seedpods open, the entire plant is cut off at ground level and hung upside down to finish drying. The beans can then be removed from the pods and stored in airtight containers.

Tips

Beans are very ornamental, with attractive leaves and plentiful flowers. Climbing beans can be grown up fences, trellises, obelisks and poles to create a screen or feature planting. Bush beans can be used to make low, temporary hedges or can be planted in small groups in the border.

Recommended

P. coccineus (runner bean) is a vigorous climbing plant, with red or sometimes white or bicoloured flowers. **'Scarlet Runner'** has bright red flowers and is one of the best and best-known cultivars. The beans can be eaten with the pod when they are young and tender, or they can be left to mature, and the pink and purple spotted beans can be dried. Plants produce edible beans in 70 days but need about 100 days for dry beans.

P. lunatus (lima bean) may be climbing or bush, depending on the cultivar. The beans are eaten as immature seeds and should be picked when the pods are plump, but the seeds are still tender. They take 70–85 days to mature. **'Fordhook'** is a popular bush variety, and **'King of the Garden'** is a good climbing selection.

P. vulgaris (wax bean, green bean, bush bean, snap bean, dry bean) is probably the largest group of beans and includes bush beans and pole beans. Some are eaten immature in the pod, and others are grown to maturity and used as dry beans. Bush beans cultivars may be yellow, such as **'Gold Rush'** and **'Sunburst';** green, such as **'Ambra'** and **'Stallion';** or purple-podded, such as **'Royal Burgundy.'** Purple beans turn bright green when cooked. Bush beans take 50–60 days to mature. Pole beans, such as **'Blue Lake'** and **'Kentucky Blue'** take 50–55 days to mature. Dry beans are usually bush plants and take about 100 days to mature. They include kidney, pinto and navy beans. A popular selection for home growers is the red and white spotted **'Jacob's Cattle.'**

Problems and Pests

Pick beans only when plants are dry to reduce the spread of disease. Problems with leaf spot, bacterial blight, rust, bean beetles and aphids can occur. Disease-infected plants should be destroyed, not composted, once you've harvested what you can.

Climbing beans are popular among gardeners with limited space because you can get more beans for less space.

P. coccineus 'Scarlet Runner' (above & below)

Beets

Beta

Features: clump-forming biennials, grown as annuals; attractive leaves; edible red, yellow or red-and-white-ringed root **Height:** 20–45 cm (8–18") **Spread:** 10–30 cm (4–12")

Beets are versatile vegetables. The plump, rounded or cylindrical roots are most commonly eaten. The tops are also edible and can be compared in flavour to spinach and Swiss chard. Beets and Swiss chard are closely related, both being members of the genus *Beta*.

B. vulgaris (above & below)

Starting

The corky, wrinkled seed of the beet is actually a dry fruit that contains several tiny seeds. Plant it directly in the garden around the last frost date. Even if you space the seeds 7–15 cm (3–6") apart, you will probably have to thin a bit because several plants can sprout from each fruit. Beets are fairly quick to mature, and a second crop can often be planted in mid-summer for an autumn crop.

Growing

Beets grow well in **full sun** or **partial shade**. They grow best in cool weather. The soil should be **fertile, moist** and **well drained**. Mulch lightly with compost to maintain moisture and improve soil texture.

Harvesting

Beets mature in 45–80 days, depending on the variety. Short-season beets are best for immediate eating and preserving, and long-season beets are the better choice for storing.

Pick beets as soon as they are big enough to eat. They are tender when young but can become woody as they mature.

You can pick leaves from the beets without pulling up the entire beet if you want to use the leaves for fresh or steamed greens. Don't pull all the leaves off a beet; just remove a few at a time from any one plant.

Tips

Beets have attractive red-veined, dark green foliage. These plants look good when planted in small groups in a border, and they make interesting edging plants. They can even be included in large mixed container plantings.

Recommended

B. vulgaris forms a dense rosette of glossy, dark green leaves, often with deep red stems and veins. It grows 20–45 cm (8–18") tall and spreads 10–20 cm (4–8"). There are many cultivars available. **'Chioggia'** is an heirloom cultivar that produces red-and-white-ringed roots. **'Detroit Dark Red'** is dark red and was developed from the heirloom **'Detroit.'** **'Early Wonder'** and **'Red Ace'** are good, red, round cultivars. **'Golden Detroit'** has red skin and yellow flesh. **'Pablo'** is a bright red baby beet. **'Rodina'** has a red, cylin-drical root.

Problems and Pests

Beets are generally problem free, but occasional trouble with scab, root maggots and flea beetles can occur.

Never fear if you get beet juice on your clothing; it won't stain. Dyers have been unsuccessfully trying to find a fixative for beet juice for centuries. Chemists inform us that the red molecule in the beet is very large and doesn't adhere to other molecules, so a fixative is unlikely to ever be found.

Blueberries

Vaccinium

Features: deciduous shrub; edible fruit; small, bell-shaped white or pink flowers; attractive habit; bright red autumn colour **Height:** 10 cm–1.5 m (4"–5')
Spread: 30 cm–1.5 m (1–5')

These attractive bushes are low and spreading, or rounded and upright. The leaves turn a beautiful shade of red in autumn. These plants are an admirable addition to any border, with the added asset of delicious summer fruit.

Starting

Plants can be purchased and planted at any time, as long as the ground is workable. The best selection is generally in spring.

Growing

Blueberries grow well in **full sun, partial shade** or **light shade**. The soil should be of **average fertility, acidic, moist** and **well drained**. Blueberries grow best in areas where the soil is acidic and peaty or sandy. The soil can be amended, but plants never grow as well in alkaline soil.

Harvesting

Blueberries are ready for harvesting when they turn, not surprisingly, blue. Test one, and if it is sweet and tastes the way you expect, they are ready for harvest.

V. angustifolium

Tips

If you have naturally acidic soil, blueberries make an excellent choice for a fruit-bearing shrub in a woody or mixed border. They are hardy in many Canadian gardens and make interesting low hedges.

Recommended

V. angustifolium var. *laevifolium* (lowbush blueberry, wild blueberry) is a low, bushy, spreading shrub with small, glossy green leaves that turn red in autumn. It grows 10–60 cm (4–24") tall and spreads 30–60 cm (12–24").

Clusters of small bell-shaped white or pink flowers are produced in spring, followed by small round fruit that ripens to dark blue in mid-summer. (Zones 2–8)

V. corymbosum (highbush blueberry) is a bushy, upright, arching shrub with green leaves that turn red or yellow in autumn. It grows 90 cm–1.5 m (3–5') tall with an equal spread. Clusters of white or pink flowers at the ends of the branches in spring are followed by berries that ripen to bright blue in

V. corymbosum

summer. Several cultivars are available, including **'Bluecrop,'** with tart, light blue berries; **'Blueray,'** with large, dark blue berries; and **'Chippewa,'** with sweet, light blue berries. (Zones 3–8)

Problems and Pests

Rare problems with caterpillars, rust, scale, powdery mildew and root rot can occur.

A handy way to preserve blueberries is to spread them on a cookie sheet and put them in a freezer. Once they are frozen, they can be put into an airtight bag and kept in the freezer. The berries will be frozen individually, rather than in a solid block, making it easy to measure out just what you need for a single recipe or serving.

Borage

Borago

Features: bushy, bristly annual; edible blue, purple or white summer flowers; bristly, edible leaves **Height:** 45–70 cm (18–28") **Spread:** 45–60 cm (18–24")

Borage leaves and flowers are both edible, making an interesting addition to salads. The flowers can also be frozen in ice cubes or used to decorate cakes and other desserts.

Starting

Seed can be sown directly in the garden in spring. This plant resents being transplanted because it has long taproots, but it recovers fairly quickly if moved when young.

Growing

Borage grows well in **full sun** or **partial shade**. The soil should be of **average fertility, light** and **well drained,** but this plant adapts to most conditions. It makes a good choice in a dry location, because it doesn't require much water to thrive.

Borage is a vigorous self-seeder. Once you have established it in your garden, you will never have to plant it again. Young seedlings can be pulled up if they are growing where you don't want them.

Harvesting

Pick borage leaves when they are young and fuzzy—they become rather bristly as they mature. Flowers can be picked any time after they open; they tend to change colour from blue to pinkish mauve as they mature.

Tips

Borage makes an attractive addition to herb and vegetable gardens, as well as to flower beds and borders. The plant should be pinched back when it is young to encourage bushy growth, otherwise it tends to flop over and develop a sprawling habit.

Recommended

B. officinalis is a bushy plant with bristly leaves and stems. It bears clusters of star-shaped, blue or purple flowers from mid-summer to autumn. A white-flowered variety is available.

Problems and Pests

Rare outbreaks of powdery mildew and aphids are possible but don't seem to be detrimental to the plant.

Borage attracts bees, butterflies and other pollinators and beneficial insects to the garden.

Broccoli

Brassica

Features: bushy, upright annual; dense clusters of edible flowers; powdery, blue-green foliage **Height:** 30–90 cm (12–36") **Spread:** 30–45 cm (12–18")

Although usually thought of as a vegetable, broccoli could more accurately be called an edible flower. It is the large, dense flower clusters that are generally eaten, though the stems and leaves are also edible.

Starting

Broccoli can be started from seed indoors or planted directly into the garden. Sow seeds indoors four to six weeks before the last frost date, and plant seedlings out or direct sow into the garden around the last frost date.

Growing

Broccoli grows best in **full sun**. The soil should be **fertile, moist** and **well drained**. Broccoli performs best in cooler weather. Mix compost into the soil, and add a layer of mulch to keep the soil moist. Don't let this plant dry out excessively because it can delay flowering.

Harvesting

Broccoli forms a central head (broccoli), and some varieties also produce side shoots. Pick the heads by cutting them cleanly from the plant with a sharp knife. If you leave them for too long on the plant, the bright yellow flowers will open.

Choosing a side-shoot-producing plant verses a main-head-only variety is a matter of personal preference. If you have a large family or plan to freeze some florets, you may prefer a large-headed selection. If there are only a few people in the household, or you want to enjoy the broccoli for longer without storing any, you may prefer the small-headed varieties that produce plenty of side shoots.

Tips

Broccoli, with its blue-green foliage, is an interesting accent plant. Tuck it in groups of three or so into your borders and mixed beds for a striking contrast. This plant is susceptible to quite a few pest and disease problems, and spacing it out rather than planting it in rows helps reduce the severity of the potential problems.

Recommended

B. oleracea var. *botrytis* is an upright plant with a stout, central, leafy stem. Flowers form at the top of the plant and sometimes from side shoots that emerge from just above each leaf. Plants grow 30–90 cm (12–36") tall and spread 30–45 cm (12–18"). Maturity dates vary from

45 to 70 days. **'Calbrese'** ('Calabria') produces plenty of side shoots. **'De Cicco'** has edible leaves and produces many side shoots. **'Gypsy'** produces a large central head and is one of the most heat-tolerant cultivars. **'Nutri-Bud'** is an early maturing cultivar that produces plenty of side shoots after the main head is cut. **'Premium Crop'** is an All America Selections winner that is early to mature and produces plenty of side shoots.

Problems and Pests

Problems with cutworms, leaf miners, caterpillars, root maggots, cabbage white butterflies, white rust, downy mildew and powdery mildew can occur. Avoid planting this plant in the same spot twice in successive years.

Cabbage white butterflies are common pests for all members of the Brassica *family, and their tiny green caterpillar larvae can be tough to spot in a head of broccoli. Break heads into pieces, and soak them in salted water for 10 or so minutes before cooking. This kills the larvae and causes them to float to the surface.*

Brussels Sprouts

Brassica

Features: bushy, upright plant, grown as an annual; fat, edible buds sprout from leaf bases along the stem; blue-green foliage **Height:** 60 cm (24")
Spread: 45 cm (18")

Love them or hate them, Brussels sprouts are at the very least a garden curiosity. Developing a stout central stem, the sprouts form on the stem at the base of each leaf. By autumn, the display is unique and eye-catching.

Starting

Brussels sprouts can be purchased as small transplants in spring, or seeds can be started indoors about six weeks before you expect to transplant them into the garden. Sowing the seeds into peat pots or pellets makes it easy to transplant the seedlings into the garden.

Growing

Brussels sprouts grow well in **full sun**. The soil should be **fertile, moist** and **well drained**. Brussels sprouts need a fairly long growing season to produce sprouts of any appreciable size, so they should be planted out as early as possible. Regular moisture also encourages them to mature quickly, so keep the soil well mulched. Once you see sprouts starting to form, you may wish to remove some of the stem leaves to give the sprouts more room to grow.

Harvesting

Pick sprouts as soon as they are large and plump, but before they begin to open. A light frost can improve the flavour of the sprouts. The entire plant can be pulled up, and if you remove the roots, leaves and top of the plant,

Nutrient rich and fibre-packed, Brussels sprouts deserve a more prominent place on our plates. People who complain that sprouts are mushy or bitter have proba-bly had ones that were poorly prepared. When picked after a light frost, steamed so that they are cooked just through to the centre and served with butter, they are delicious. You can also steam them in the oven to bring out their sweetness.

To avoid overcooking Brussels sprouts, cut an X in the stem about one-quarter of the way through each sprout to help the inside cook at the same rate as the outside.

the sprouts can be stored on the stem in a cool place for up to four weeks. Be sure to keep an eye on them because they can go bad quickly. They can also be frozen for later use.

Tips

Brussels sprouts create a leafy back-drop for your flowering annuals and perennials all summer; then, just as the garden is fading, they create an interesting focal point as the plump little sprouts develop.

Recommended

B. oleracea* var. *gemnifera is an upright plant that develops a single leafy stem. Sprouts form at the base of each leaf along the stem. The leaves are blue-green, often with white mid-ribs and stems. **'Bedford Fillbasket,' 'Jade Cross'** and **'Vancouver'** are popular cultivars.

Problems and Pests

Problems with cutworms, leaf miners, caterpillars, root maggots, aphids, cabbage white butterfly larvae, white rust, downy mildew and powdery mildew can occur.

Cabbage

Brassica

Features: biennial, grown as an annual; dense, round, red, purple, blue-green or green, leafy clumps; smooth or crinkled leaves **Height:** 45–60 cm (18–24") **Spread:** 30–45 cm (12–18")

Cabbages are easy to grow, and they create a dense, leafy, often colourful display. They come in three forms: green with smooth leaves, green with very crinkled leaves and red or purple, usually with smooth leaves.

Starting

Start seeds indoors about four weeks before you plan to transplant them outdoors. You can also direct sow them into the garden around the last frost date as long as the soil has warmed up a bit.

Growing

Cabbages grow best in **full sun**. They prefer cool growing conditions and benefit from mulch to retain moisture during hot weather. The soil should be **fertile, moist** and **well drained**.

Harvesting

The leaves of young plants can be eaten. When a good-sized head has developed, cut it cleanly from the plant. Smaller heads often develop once the main head has been cut. Plants are frost hardy, and the last of the cabbages can be left in the ground through fall, then stored in a cold, frost-free location. Cabbages that take a long time to mature generally store better than quick-maturing types.

Tips

Choose a variety of cabbages because the different colours, textures and maturing times create a more interesting display, whether in rows or mixed into your borders.

Recommended

B. oleracea var. *capitata* is a low, leafy rosette that develops a dense head over summer. Leaves may be green, blue-green, red or purple and smooth or crinkled. It matures in 60–140 days, depending on the variety. Some popular smooth-leaved, green varieties are '**January**

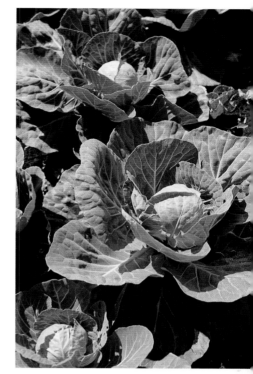

King,' 'Bartolo,' 'Early Jersey Wakefield,' 'Lennox' and 'Parel.' Popular crinkled or savoy types include '**Savoy Blue,' 'Savoy King,' 'Taler'** and '**Wirosa.'** Popular red cabbages include '**Buscaro,' 'Red Acre Early,' 'Red Drumhead,' 'Red Express'** and '**Ruby Dynasty.'**

Problems and Pests

Problems with cutworms, leaf miners, caterpillars, root maggots, aphids, cabbage white butterfly larvae, white rust, downy mildew and powdery mildew can occur.

Don't forget that all members of the cabbage family (Brassica) are susceptible to many of the same pests and diseases. Don't plant them in the same spot two years in a row, particularly if you've had disease problems in that area.

Calendula
Pot Marigold, English marigold
Calendula

Features: hardy annual; edible, yellow, orange, cream, gold or apricot flowers; long blooming period **Height:** 25–60 cm (10–24") **Spread:** 20–50 cm (8–20")

Bright and charming, calendula produces attractive, brightly coloured flowers in summer and autumn.

Starting

Calendula grows easily from seed. Sprinkle the seeds where you want them to grow (they don't like to be transplanted), and cover them lightly with soil. They will sprout within a week.

Young plants are often difficult to find in nurseries because this plant is so quick and easy to start from seed.

Growing

Calendula does equally well in **full sun** or **partial shade**. The soil should be of **average fertility** and **well drained**. Calendula likes cool weather and can withstand a moderate frost. Deadhead the plant to prolong blooming and keep it looking neat. If your plant fades in the summer heat, cut it back to 10–15 cm (4–6") above the ground to encourage new growth. A fading plant can also be pulled up and new seeds planted. Both methods provide a good autumn display.

Harvesting

Flowers can be picked as needed for fresh use, or the petals can be dried for later use.

Tips

This informal plant looks attractive in borders and mixed in among vegetables or other plants. It can also be used in mixed planters and container gardens. Calendula is a cold-hardy annual and often continues flowering, even through a layer of snow, until the ground freezes completely.

Recommended

C. officinalis is a vigorous, tough, upright plant that grows 30–60 cm

C. officinalis

(12–24") tall and spreads 25–50 cm (10–20"). It bears single or double, daisy-like flowers in a wide range of yellow and orange shades. **'Bon Bon'** is a dwarf plant that grows 25–30 cm (10–12") tall and bears flowers in shades of yellow, orange and apricot. **'Pacific Beauty'** is an heirloom cultivar with large, brightly coloured flowers. It grows 45–60 cm (18–24") tall. **'Victoria Sunset'** bears large, double, burnt orange flowers on plants that grow 45–60 cm (18–24") tall.

Problems and Pests

Calendula is usually trouble free. It continues to perform well even when afflicted with rare problems such as aphids, whiteflies, smut, powdery mildew and fungal leaf spot.

Calendula flowers are popular kitchen herbs that can be added to stews for colour or to salads for flavour.

Caraway

Carum

Features: hardy biennial; feathery, light green foliage; clusters of tiny white flowers; edible seeds **Height:** 20–60 cm (8–24") **Spread:** 30 cm (12")

In use for over 5000 years, caraway is a tasty addition to savoury and sweet dishes. The seeds are used in sauerkraut, stews, rye bread, pies and coleslaw.

C. carvi

Starting

Caraway can be started from seed and should be planted where you want it to grow because it can bolt (go to flower) quickly when the roots are disturbed.

Growing

Caraway grows best in **full sun**, but tolerates some shade. The soil should be **fertile, loose** and **well drained**. This plant is biennial and generally doesn't bloom until the second year. It is a vigorous self-seeder.

Harvesting

Cut the ripe seedheads from the plants, and place them in a paper bag. Loosely tie the bag closed, and hang it in a dry location. Once the seeds are dry, they can be stored in an airtight jar. The seedheads are ripe when the seedpods just begin to open.

Tips

Caraway hasn't got a very strong presence in the garden, but it can be planted in groups with more decorative plants where its ferny foliage and pretty white flowers add a delicate, airy touch.

Recommended

C. carvi is a delicate-looking, upright biennial with ferny foliage. In the second summer after sowing, white flowers are borne in flat-topped clusters. This plant is dependably hardy to zone 5 and can be overwintered in colder gardens with a good mulch in fall.

Problems and Pests

Caraway rarely suffers from any pests or problems.

Planting caraway near your cabbages will attract predatory insects and will also help you to remember to add some caraway seed to your cabbage as it cooks. Caraway helps to reduce the cooking odour and the flatulence that can be a by-product of eating cabbage.

Carrots

Daucus

Features: biennial, grown as an annual; feathery foliage; edible root
Height: 20–45 cm (8–18") **Spread:** 5–10 cm (2–4")

Just about anyone who has grown vegetables in the past remembers pulling a carrot out of the garden, brushing the dirt off and munching on it with the greens still attached. This simple pleasure is one of my favourite parts of growing my own vegetables.

Starting

Carrots can be sown directly into the garden once the last frost date has passed and the soil has warmed up. The seeds are very tiny and can be difficult to plant evenly. Mix the tiny seeds with sand before you sow them to spread the seeds more evenly and reduce the need for thinning. You can also purchase seeds that have been coated with clay to make them easier to handle. Cover only very lightly with sand or compost when planting, because the seeds can't sprout through too much soil. Keep the seedbed moist to encourage even germination.

Growing

Carrots grow best in **full sun**. The soil should be **average to fertile, well drained** and **deeply prepared**. Because you are growing carrots for the root, you need to be sure that the soil is loose and free of rocks to a depth of 20–30 cm (8–12"). This gives carrots plenty of space to develop and makes them easier to pull up when they are ready for eating. If your soil is very rocky or shallow, you may wish to plant carrots in raised beds to provide deeper, looser soil, or grow shorter varieties of carrots.

Spacing carrots is a gradual process. As the carrots develop, pull a few of the more crowded ones out, leaving room for the others to fill in. This thinning process will give you an indication of how well they are developing and when they are ready to harvest. The root can be eaten at all stages of development.

Harvesting

Never judge carrots by their greens. Big, bushy tops are no indication that carrots are ready for picking. As the roots develop, you will often see the top of the carrots at or just above soil level—a better indication of their development. You can pull carrots up by getting a good grip on the greens in loose enough soil, but you may need a small garden hand fork or large fork to dig them up in a heavier soil.

Tips

Carrots make an excellent ornamental grouping or edging plant. The feathery foliage provides an attractive background for flowers and plants with ornamental foliage.

Recommended

D. carota var. sativus forms a bushy mound of feathery foliage. It matures in 50–75 days. The edible roots may be orange, red, yellow, white or purple. They come in a variety of shapes, from long and slender to short and round. The type you choose will depend on the flavour you like, how long you need to store them and how suitable your soil is. **'Little Finger'** produces baby carrots.

'Napoli' is an early maturing, sweet carrot. **'Purple Haze'** has purple-skinned, orange-fleshed carrots. **'Rainbow'** produces roots in white, yellow and several shades of orange. **'Resistafly'** is rust fly resistant. **'Royal Chantenay'** is an heirloom carrot with a deep orange core. **'Scarlet Nantes'** ('Nantes') is a sweet heirloom carrot.

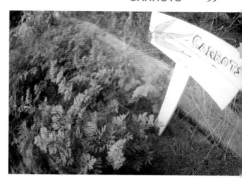

Problems and Pests

Carrot rust flies and root maggots can sometimes be troublesome.

To keep carrots for a long time, it is best to store them in a cold, frost-free place in containers of moistened sand.

Cauliflower

Brassica

Features: annual; white, purple, green, yellow or orange, edible flowerheads
Height: 45–60 cm (18–24") **Spread:** 45 cm (18")

With the interesting assortment of colours now available, cauliflower can create quite an interesting display in the late-summer or fall garden. Tuck a few here and there in your mixed borders.

Starting

Cauliflower can be sown directly into the garden around the last frost date, or you can start them indoors about four weeks before you plan to set them outdoors.

Growing

Cauliflower grows best in **full sun**. The soil should be **fertile, moist** and **well drained**. This plant doesn't like persistently hot weather (more than two weeks with temperatures over 28° C [80° F]), rarely a problem, even in comparatively hot Canadian gardens. Cauliflower must have a rich soil that stays evenly moist, or heads may form poorly, if at all. Mix plenty of compost into the soil, and mulch with compost to help keep the soil moist.

Harvesting

Unlike broccoli, cauliflower does not develop secondary heads once the main one is cut. Cut the head cleanly from the plant when it is mature. You can then compost the plant.

Tips

White cauliflower may turn yellow or greenish unless some of the leaves are tied over the head to shade it from the sun. Tie some of the outer leaves together over the head with elastic or string when you first notice it forming.

Purple cauliflower generally turns green when cooked. Unlike white cauliflower, the purple-, green-, yellow- or orange-headed varieties need no shading while they develop.

Recommended

B. oleracea var. *botrytis* is leafy and upright with dense, edible flower clusters in the centre of the plant. Most selections take 70–85 days to mature, though some mature in as few as 45 days. Popular white-headed cultivars include **'Early Dawn,' 'Snowball'** and **'Symphony.' 'Graffiti'** and **'Violet Queen'** are purple-headed cultivars. **'Green Harmony'** and **'Veronica'** are green-headed cultivars, with Veronica's florets forming pointed tapering peaks. **'Cheddar'** is an orange-headed cultivar.

Problems and Pests

Problems with cutworms, leaf miners, caterpillars, root maggots, aphids, cabbage white butterfly larvae, white rust, downy mildew and powdery mildew can occur.

Celery · Celeriac

Apium

Features: biennial, grown as an annual; bright green leaves; bushy habit; edible stems **Height:** 45 cm (18") **Spread:** 25 cm (10")

Tender ribbed stalks of celery fresh from the garden are quite different than store-bought celery. The flavour of unblanched stems is much stronger but much appreciated by many gardeners.

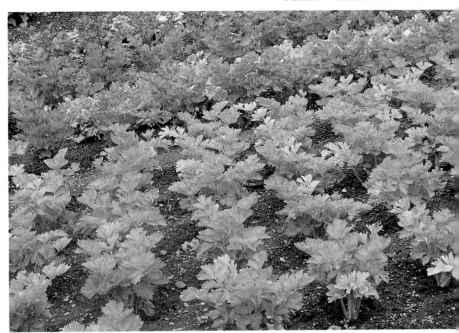

Starting

Celery seed should be started indoors at least eight weeks and up to 12 weeks before you plan to transplant it outdoors. Be patient; seed can take up to three weeks to germinate. Be sure to keep the planting medium moist, but not soggy. Avoid planting out until the last frost date has passed and the soil has warmed up. Mulch plants to conserve moisture.

Growing

Celery and celeriac grow best in **full sun**, but enjoy light or afternoon shade in hot weather. The soil should be **fertile, humus rich, moist** and **well drained**. Allowing the soil to dry out too much will give you a poor quality, bad-tasting vegetable. In late summer, you can mound soil around the celery stalks or wrap them in newspaper to shade them from the sun and encourage the development of the pale green or blanched stems we are familiar with. Unblanched stalks have a stronger flavour that some people prefer. Celeriac needs no blanching.

Harvesting

Celery stalks can be harvested one or two at a time from each plant for most of summer. If you are blanching the stems before picking all or some of them, they will be ready for harvesting two or three weeks after the stalks are covered. A light touch of frost can sweeten the flavour of the celery.

Celeriac should be harvested before the first autumn frost. Pull plants up, remove the leaves and store the knobby roots the same way you would beets, in a cold, frost-free location in a container of moistened sand.

Tips

Celery and celeriac have light green leaves that create a very bushy back-drop for flowering plants with less attractive, spindly growth.

Recommended

A. graveolens var. *dulce* (celery) is a bushy, upright plant with attractive, light to bright green foliage. It matures in 100–120 days. **'Celery XP 266,' 'Conquistador,' 'Golden Self-Blanching,' 'Red Stalk'** and **'Utah 52-70'** are popular cultivars.

Blanching is a gardening technique usually used on bitter-tasting vegetables. Partially or completely depriving the plant of light sweetens the flavour. Though many devices have been developed to make blanching easier, a good mound of soil or mulch will do the job just fine.

A. graveolens var. *rapaceum* (cele-riac) forms a bushy, bright green plant that develops a thick knobby, bulbous root. It matures in 100–120 days. **'Diamant'** and **'Giant Prague'** are popular cultivars.

Problems and Pests

Problems with fungal blight, mosaic virus, *fusarium* yellows, bacterial and fungal rot, leaf spot and caterpillars can occur.

Cold nights can cause celery to flower, leaving the stalks inedible, or at least unpalatable.

Chamomile

Matricaria

Features: bushy annual; fragrant feathery foliage; daisy-like flowers can be used to make tea **Height:** 30–60 cm (12–24") **Spread:** 15–20 cm (6–8")

Chamomile's pretty, flavourful flowers can be used to make a perfect after-dinner tea. This delicate and airy plant is useful for filling in garden spaces wherever it is planted.

M. recutita (above & below)

Starting

Seeds can be started about four weeks early indoors or sown directly in the garden once the last frost date has passed.

Growing

Chamomile grows best in **full sun**. The soil should be of **average fertility, sandy** and **well drained**. Chamomile self-seeds freely if you don't pick all the flowers.

Harvesting

As the flowers mature, the petals fall off and the centres swell as the seeds start to develop. At this point, the flowers can be picked and used fresh or dried for tea.

Tips

Chamomile is an attractive plant to use along the edge of a pathway or to edge beds where the fragrance will be released when the foliage is brushed against, bruised or crushed. The flowers attract beneficial insects, so you may also want to plant a few here and there among your other plants.

Chamomile tea is a relaxing beverage to have before bed or after a meal to help settle the stomach.

Recommended

M. recutita (German chamomile) is an upright annual with soft, finely divided, fern-like foliage and bears small, daisy-like flowers in summer. It grows 30–60 cm (12–24") tall and spreads 15–20 cm (6–8").

Problems and Pests

Chamomile rarely suffers from any problems.

Chard · Swiss Chard

Beta

Features: biennial, grown as an annual; glossy green, purple, red or bronze, edible foliage; green, white, yellow, orange, pink, red or purple stems and veins
Height: 20–45 cm (8–18") **Spread:** 30 cm (12")

Chard is one of the most useful vegetables to include in your garden. The tasty leaves and stems can be harvested all summer, and the wide range of colours makes it a valuable ornamental addition to beds, borders and even container gardens.

Starting

The corky wrinkled seed of chard is actually a dry fruit that contains several tiny seeds. Plant the dry fruit directly in the garden around the last frost date. Even if you space the seeds 7–15 cm (3–6") apart, you will probably have to thin a bit, because several plants can sprout from each fruit.

Growing

Chard grows well in **full sun** or **partial shade**. It grows best in cool weather. The soil should be **fertile, moist** and **well drained**. Mulch lightly with compost to maintain moisture and improve soil texture.

Harvesting

Chard matures quickly, and a few leaves can be plucked from each plant every week or so all summer. You can generally start picking leaves about a month after the seed sprouts and continue to do so until the plant is killed back by frost.

Tips

Chard has very decorative foliage. Though the leaves are all generally glossy green, the stems and veins are often brightly coloured in shades of red, pink, white, yellow or orange. When

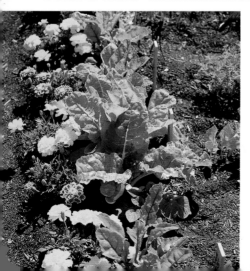

planted in small groups in your borders, chard adds a colourful touch. The bushy, clumping habit also makes it well suited to mixed container plantings.

Recommended

B. vulgaris* subsp. *cicla forms a clump of glossy green, purple, red or bronze leaves that are often deeply crinkled or savoyed. Stems and veins may be pale green, white, yellow, orange, pink, red or purple. Plants grow 20–45 cm (8–18") tall and spread about 30 cm (12").

Popular cultivars include '**Fordhook Giant,**' a white-stemmed heirloom; '**Orange Fantasia,**' with orange stems; '**Perpetual,**' a non-bolting, heat-resistant cultivar with pale green stems; '**Rainbow,**' with a combination of red, orange, yellow or white stems; '**Rhubarb,**' with bright red stems; and '**Silverado,**' with creamy white stems.

Problems and Pests

Rare problems with downy mildew, powdery mildew, leaf miners, aphids, caterpillars and root rot can occur.

If you find that chard fades out in your garden during the heat of summer, you can plant a second crop in mid-summer for fresh leaves in late summer and autumn.

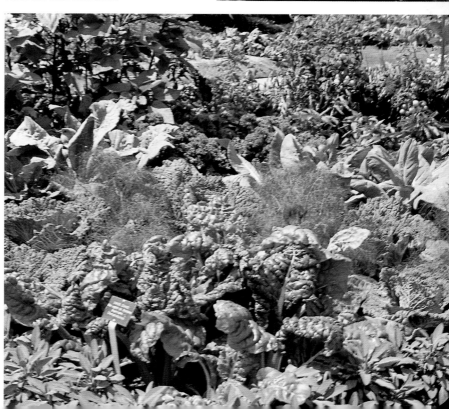

Chives

Allium

Features: foliage; habit; mauve, pink or white flowers **Height:** 20–60 cm (8–24")
Spread: 30 cm (12") or more

The delicate onion flavour of chives is best enjoyed fresh. Mix chives
into dips, or sprinkle them on salads
and baked potatoes. The
blooms are striking in
the garden and in
salads and herbal
vinegars.

A. schoenoprasum

Starting

Chives can be started indoors four to six weeks before the last frost date or can be planted directly in the garden. They can also be purchased as plants.

Growing

Chives grow best in **full sun**. The soil should be **fertile, moist** and **well drained,** but chives adapt to most soil conditions. Plants self-seed freely in good growing conditions. The youngest leaves are the most tender and flavourful, so cut plants back to encourage new growth if flavour diminishes over summer.

Harvesting

Chives can be snipped off with scissors all spring, summer and fall, as needed. Flowers are usually used just after they open, and the individual flowers in the cluster are broken apart for use.

Tips

Chives are decorative enough to be included in a mixed or herbaceous border and can be left to naturalize. In an herb garden, chives should be given plenty of space to allow for self-seeding.

Recommended

A. schoenoprasum (chives) forms a clump of bright green, cylindrical leaves. Clusters of pinkish purple flowers are produced in early and midsummer. Varieties with white or pink flowers are also available. (Zones 3–8)

A. tuberosum (garlic chives) forms a clump of long, narrow, flat, dark green leaves. Clusters of white flowers are borne all summer. The young leaves have a distinctive garlic flavour. They are even more prone to self-seeding than chives. (Zones 3–8)

Problems and Pests

Chives rarely have any problems.

Chives are said to increase appetite and encourage good digestion.

Coriander · Cilantro

Coriandrum

Features: habit; foliage; flowers; seeds **Height:** 45–60 cm (18–24")
Spread: 20–45 cm (8–18")

Coriander is a multi-purpose herb. The leaves, called cilantro, are used in salads, salsas and soups. The seeds, called coriander, are used in cakes, pies, chutneys and marmalades. The flavour of each is quite distinct.

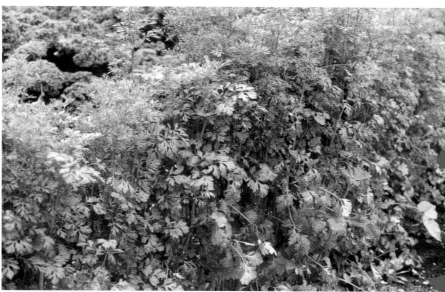
C. sativum

Starting

Coriander can be started from seed four to six weeks before the last frost date or sown directly in the garden. Started plants can also be purchased from nurseries, garden centres or herb specialists. Several smaller sowings two weeks apart will ensure a steady supply of leaves.

Growing

Coriander prefers **full sun** but benefits from afternoon shade during the heat of summer in hotter parts of Canada. The soil should be **fertile, light** and **well drained**. This plant dislikes humid conditions and does best during a dry summer.

Harvesting

Leaves can be harvested as needed throughout summer. Seeds can be harvested as they ripen in autumn. Spread out a large sheet and shake the seedheads over it to collect the seeds.

Tips

Coriander has pungent leaves and is best planted where people who don't appreciate the scent won't have to brush past it. The plant is a delight to behold when in flower. Add a plant here and there throughout your borders, both for the visual appeal and to attract beneficial insects.

Recommended

C. sativum is an annual herb that forms a clump of lacy basal foliage, above which large, loose clusters of tiny, white flowers are produced. The seeds ripen in late summer and fall.

Problems and Pests

This plant rarely suffers from any problems.

Coriander is one of the best plants for attracting predatory insects to your garden.

Corn

Zea

Features: annual grass; broad, strap-shaped leaves; tassel-like flowers
Height: 1.2–2.4 m (4–8') **Spread:** 30–60 cm (12–24")

Corn is believed to have originated in South America. Widely grown by Native peoples in both North and South America, corn is one of the 'Three Sisters' of native gardens. Corn, beans and squash were grown together as companions. The beans fixed nitrogen in the soil and could climb up the corn for support. The large leaves of squash shaded the soil and kept weeds to a minimum.

Starting

Start seed directly in the garden once the last frost date has passed and the soil has warmed; seed will rot in too cool a soil. Depending on the variety you choose, corn can take from 75 to 110 days to mature. If your growing season is short or the soil is slow to warm, you may prefer to start your corn four to six weeks early in peat pots and transplant it to the garden after the last frost date.

Growing

Corn grows best in **full sun**. The soil should be **fertile, moist** and **well drained**. As the plant develops, you can mound more soil around its base; the stem will develop roots in this soil, and the plant will be stronger and less likely to blow over in a strong wind.

There are ornamental varieties of corn available; some, such as 'Fiesta' and 'Seneca Indian,' have colourful kernels on the cobs; others, such as 'Harlequin' and 'Variegata,' have foliage striped in red, green and white or creamy white, respectively.

Harvesting

Corn is ready to pick when the silks start to turn brown and the kernels are plump. If you peel the husk back just slightly, you will be able to see if the kernels are plump and the corn is ready for harvest. Heirloom varieties should be picked and used as quickly as possible because they begin to turn starchy as soon as they are picked. Newer selections have had their genes modified to increase their sweetness and ability to stay sweet after picking. These can be stored for a while with no loss of sweetness.

Avoid growing both popcorn and sweet corn, or keep them well separated, to avoid cross-pollination, which can make both inedible.

Tips

Corn is wind pollinated, so plants need to be fairly close together for pollination to occur. Planting in groups improves your pollination rates when you are only growing a few plants. Corn is an architectural grass that looks similar to some of the upright ornamental grasses, such as miscanthus. Plant it in groups of 5–9 in your beds and borders.

Recommended

Z. mays is a sturdy, upright grass with bright green leaves with undulating edges. Plants grow 1.2–2.4 m (4–8') and spread 30–60 cm (12–24"). **Var. *rugosa*** (sweet corn) matures in 65–80 days and falls into several sweetness categories. These gauge both how sweet the corn is and how quickly the sugar turns to starch once the corn is picked. Some of the sweeter corns are less tolerant of cold soils. Kernels can be white or yellow, or cobs may have a combination of both colours. **Var. *praecox*** (popcorn) matures in 100–110 days and has shorter cobs with hard, yellow, white or red kernels.

Problems and Pests

Corn earworms, aphids, caterpillars, downy mildew, rust, smut and fungal leaf spots can be a problem for corn.

Cucumber

Cucumis

Features: trailing or climbing annual vine; decorative leaves; yellow flowers; edible fruit **Height:** 30 cm (12"), when trailing **Spread:** 2.4–4.8 m (4–8'), when trailing

Cucumbers are popular in salads. Try a mixed container of salad plants such as tomatoes, green peppers and basil. If only we could grow olives in Canada, we'd have the perfect mixed salad planting.

C. sativus (above & below)

Starting

Cucumbers can be started indoors about four weeks before the last frost date or can be sown directly into the garden once the last frost date has passed and the soil has warmed up. If you are starting your plants indoors, plant the seeds in peat pots so the roots will not be damaged or disturbed when you transplant them outdoors.

Growing

Cucumbers grow well in **full sun** or **light shade**. The soil should be **fertile, moist** and **well drained**. Consistent moisture is most important when plants are germinating and once fruit is being produced. If you are growing your cucumbers up a trellis or other support, you will probably need to tie the vines in place. Use strips of old nylons or other soft ties to prevent damaging the plant.

Harvesting

When to harvest will depend on the kind of cucumbers you are growing. Pickling cucumbers are picked while they are young and small. Slicing cucumbers can be picked when mature or when small if you want to use them for pickling. Long and slender Oriental cucumbers are picked when mature and tend to be sweeter, developing no bitter flavour with age.

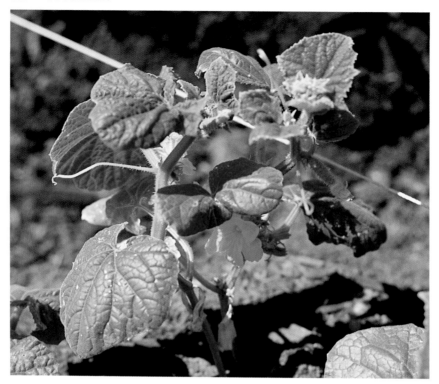

Tips

Cucumbers are versatile trailing plants. They can be left to wind their way through the other plants in your garden or grown up trellises or other supports. The mound-forming varieties also make attractive additions to a container garden.

Cucumbers keep producing fruit as long as you don't let the fruit stay on the vines for too long. Pick cucumbers as soon as they are a good size for eating. The more you pick, the more the plants will produce.

Recommended

C. sativus is a trailing annual vine with coarse-textured leaves and bristly stems. It matures in 45–60 days. Popular slicing and salad cucumbers include the long, slender **'English Telegraph'** and **'Sweet Slender'**; All America Selections winner **'Fanfare,'** a prolific bush selection; and the high-yielding **'Stonewall.'** Pickling cucumbers are harvested when small, and popular cultivars include the disease-tolerant, semi-bush **'Cross Country'** and the prolific, bushy **'Patio Pickles.'**

Wondering about the round, yellow cucumber in the photo on page 120? 'Lemon' is a heritage variety with a crisp texture and mild flavour; it's great in salads. The vines are trailing and because the fruit is not too heavy they are ideal for growing up a low trellis.

Problems and Pests

Problems with powdery mildew, downy mildew, mosaic virus, white flies, aphids, cucumber beetles, bacterial wilt, leaf spot, scab and ring spot can occur.

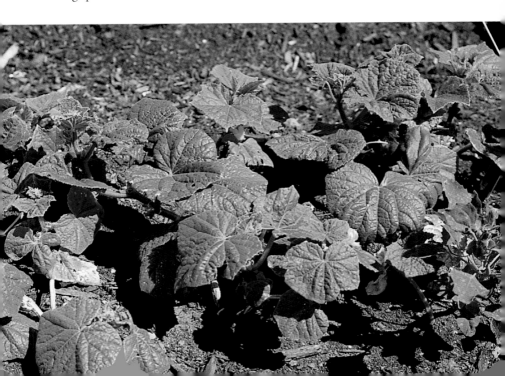

Dill

Anethum

Features: feathery, edible foliage; yellow summer flowers; edible seeds
Height: 60 cm–1.5 m (2–5') **Spread:** 30 cm (12"), or more

Dill is majestic and beautiful in any garden setting. Its leaves and seeds are probably best known for their use as pickling herbs, though they have a wide variety of other culinary uses.

Starting

Dill can be sown directly into the garden around the last frost date. Make several small sowings every couple of weeks to ensure a steady supply of leaves.

Growing

Dill grows best in **full sun** in a **sheltered** location out of strong winds. The soil should be of **poor to average fertility, moist** and **well drained**. Don't grow dill near fennel because they will cross-pollinate, and the seeds of both plants will lose their distinct flavours.

Harvesting

Pick the leaves as needed throughout summer and dry them for use in winter. Harvest the seeds by shaking the seedheads over a sheet once they ripen in late summer or fall.

Tips

With its feathery leaves, dill is an attractive addition to a mixed bed or border. It can be included in a vegetable garden but does well in any sunny location. Dill also attracts butterflies and beneficial insects to the garden.

Recommended

A. graveolens is an annual herb that forms a clump of feathery foliage. Clusters of yellow flowers are borne at the tops of sturdy stems.

Problems and Pests

Dill rarely suffers from any problems.

Eggplant
Solanum

Features: perennial, grown as an annual; bushy habit; purple or white flowers; decorative, edible fruit **Height:** 45–60 cm (18–24") **Spread:** 45 cm (18")

Eggplants are native to India and generally enjoy warmer weather than occurs naturally in most Canadian gardens. We can grow eggplant successfully by taking advantage of natural hot spots and using heat-retaining mulch.

Starting

Seeds can be started indoors six to eight weeks before the last frost date. Germination rates improve if bottom heat is used. Don't plant seedlings into the garden until the soil is warm and night temperatures stay above 15° C (60° F).

Growing

Eggplants grow best in **full sun** in a **warm, sheltered** location. The soil should be **fertile, moist** and **well drained**. Pick the warmest spot in your garden to grow these plants. Dark mulch keeps the soil warmer and reduces evaporation. Mix compost into the soil to improve fertility and moisture retention.

Harvesting

Eggplants take 50–60 days to begin producing fruit, though they can take longer in cooler Canadian gardens. Choose the shorter-season varieties for the best yields. Cut fruit cleanly from the plants with a sharp knife to prevent damage.

Tips

Eggplants develop fruit in a variety of sizes, shapes and colours. Plant several types for an interesting display and so you can sample varieties you are less familiar with. Plants are bushy and bear pretty flowers, making them a welcome addition to beds and borders.

Recommended

S. melongena var. *esculentum* is a bushy plant with small purple or white flowers. The fruit ranges in shape from small and round to long and slender and in colour from deep purple to white, with mottled

variations in between. Flavour varies significantly from cultivar to cultivar; experiment to see which grow best and which you enjoy the most. **'Baby Bell'** produces small, round, purple fruit. **'Cloud Nine'** produces pale, creamy white fruit. **'Fairy Tale'** is an All America Selections winner with long, light purple, white-streaked fruit.

Problems and Pests

Blister beetles, lace bugs, blight and potato beetles can cause problems.

Fennel
Florence Fennel
Foeniculum

Features: short-lived perennial or annual; attractive, fragrant foliage; yellow, late-summer flowers; edible seeds **Height:** 60 cm–1.8 m (2–6') **Spread:** 30–60 cm (12–24")

All parts of fennel are edible and have a distinctive, licorice-like fragrance and flavour. The seeds are commonly used to make a tea that is good for settling the stomach after a large meal. Florence fennel produces a large swollen base that is eaten raw in salads, cooked in soups and stews or roasted like other root vegetables.

Starting

Seeds can be started directly in the garden around the last frost date or about four weeks earlier indoors.

Growing

Fennel grows best in **full sun**. The soil should be **average to fertile, moist** and **well drained**. Avoid planting fennel near dill or coriander, because cross-pollination reduces seed production and makes the seed flavour of each less distinct. Fennel easily self-sows.

Harvesting

Harvest fennel leaves as needed for fresh use. The seeds can be harvested when ripe, in late summer or fall. Shake the seedheads over a sheet to collect the seeds. Let them dry thoroughly before storing them. Florence fennel can be harvested as soon as the bulbous base becomes swollen. Pull plants up as needed, and harvest any left in the ground before the first fall frost.

Tips

Fennel is an attractive addition to a mixed bed or border. The flowers attract pollinators and predatory insects to the garden.

Recommended

F. vulgare is a short-lived perennial that forms clumps of loose, feathery foliage. Clusters of small, yellow flowers are borne in late summer, followed by seeds that ripen in fall. **Var. *azoricum*** (Florence fennel, anise) is a biennial that forms a large, edible bulb at the plant base. (Zones 4–9)

Problems and Pests

Fennel rarely suffers from any problems.

Fennel bulbs combine well with many other vegetables in savoury recipes, but makes an interesting addition to sweet recipes too. Try adding some to your next fruit salad.

Fiddlehead Ferns

Matteuccia

Features: perennial fern; attractive foliage; edible, tender shoots
Height: 90 cm–1.5 m (3–5') **Spread:** 30–90 cm (12–36")

These popular, classic ferns are revered for their delicious, emerging spring fronds and their stately, vase-shaped habit.

The tightly coiled, new spring fronds taste delicious lightly steamed when served with butter. Remove the bitter, reddish brown, papery coating before steaming.

M. struthiopteris

Starting
Crowns can be purchased and planted out in spring. Plants are sometimes also available in summer. They are often sold as ornamental plants in the perennial department of your local garden centre or nursery.

Growing
Fiddlehead ferns prefer **light or partial shade** and tolerate full shade, or full sun if the soil stays moist. The soil should be **average to fertile, humus rich, neutral to acidic** and **moist**. Leaves may scorch if the soil is not moist enough. These fronds are aggressive spreaders that reproduce by spores; give them a large area to spread so you'll have plenty of fronds to harvest.

Harvesting
Let plants become established for a couple of years before you begin harvesting. Pick new fronds in spring as they are just beginning to uncurl, and be sure to pick no more than half the fronds from each plant.

Tips
These ferns appreciate a moist woodland garden and are often found growing wild alongside woodland streams and creeks. Useful in shaded borders, these plants are quick to spread.

Recommended
M. struthiopteris (*M. pennsylvanica*) forms a circular cluster of slightly arching, feathery fronds. Stiff, brown, fertile fronds, covered in reproductive spores, stick up in the centre of the cluster in late summer and persist through winter. They are popular choices for dried arrangements.

Problems and Pests
These ferns rarely suffer from any problems.

Flax

Linum

Features: upright annual; blue flowers; edible seeds **Height:** 30–90 cm (12–36")
Spread: 20–45 cm (8–18")

Flaxseed has long been added to baked muffins, breads and cereals.
It is now being hailed for its fantastic health-improving potential
and is an excellent source of omega-3 fatty acids.

*This species is not used exclusively
as a food source; the stems of some
cultivars are processed to produce
linen. Linseed oil also comes from
the seeds of flax.*

L. usitatissimum (above & below)

Starting
Start seed directly in the garden around the last frost date.

Growing
Flax grows best in **full sun**. The soil should be of **average fertility, light, humus rich** and **well drained**.

Harvesting
When they are ripe, harvest the seeds by rubbing the seedheads between your hands over a sheet or bucket. Dry the seeds completely before storing them in a cool, dry place.

Tips
Flax is a beautiful plant that many gardeners grow for its ornamental appeal alone. Each flower lasts only one day and is replaced by another each day once blooming begins.

Recommended
L. usitatissimum forms clumps with leafy, upright stems that wave at the slightest breeze. The blue summer flowers are followed by chestnut brown, pale brown or golden yellow seeds in late summer or fall.

Problems and Pests
Problems with rot, rust, wilt, slugs, snails and aphids can occur.

Garlic

Allium

Features: perennial bulb; narrow, strap-shaped leaves; white summer flowers
Height: 15–60 cm (6–24") **Spread:** 20 cm (8")

Garlic is not the most ornamental plant, but the light green leaves
make a good groundcover and repel several common garden pests.

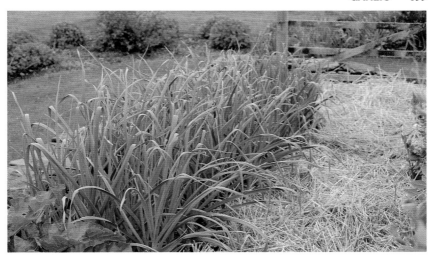

Starting

Garlic is generally grown from sets (cloves) that can be started in fall or spring. Autumn-planted garlic produces the largest bulbs at harvest time, but don't expect to see much development from this bulb until the following spring. All the autumn growth will be underground, and gives the plant a head start in spring.

Growing

Garlic grows best in **full sun**. The soil should be **fertile, moist** and **well drained**.

Harvesting

This plant can be dug up in autumn once the leaves have yellowed and died back. Softneck garlic can be stored for a longer time than hardneck varieties, but it is not as hardy.

Tips

Although the flowers are quite attractive and often intriguing, they should be removed so the plant devotes all its energy to bulb production rather than seed

production. Garlic takes up very little space and can be tucked into any spare spot in your garden.

Recommended

A. sativum var. *ophioscordon* (hardneck garlic) has a stiff central stem around which the cloves develop.

A. sativum var. *sativum* (softneck garlic) develops more cloves but has no stiff stem. The soft leaves are often used to braid garlic bulbs together for storage.

Problems and Pests

A few rot problems can occur, but this plant is generally trouble free.

Horseradish

Armoracia

Features: clump-forming perennial; pungent edible root; glossy green, creased leaves **Height:** 60–90 cm (2–3') **Spread:** 45 cm (18"), or more

Horseradish is another plant that is too often relegated to a neglected back corner of the garden. Despite its rampant ability to spread, it has beautiful foliage that makes it a prime candidate for perennial and mixed borders.

Horseradish sauce is a popular garnish for roasted meats, roast beef in particular.

A. rusticana (below)

Starting

Plants can be purchased, or if you know someone with a horseradish plant, they can give you a division or a piece of root. As with dandelions, a new plant will generally grow from even a small piece of root.

Growing

Horseradish grows well in **full sun**. The soil should be **fertile, moist** and **well drained**, but the plant adapts to most conditions.

Harvesting

When the foliage dies back in autumn, you can dig up some of the roots to use fresh or in preserves, relishes and pickles. The roots have the strongest flavour in autumn, but they can be harvested at any time once the plant is well established.

Tips

Horseradish is a vigorous plant that spreads to form a sizeable clump. It is fairly adaptable and can be used in a somewhat neglected area, but it deserves a better spot because of its glossy, creased foliage.

Recommended

A. rusticana forms a large, spreading clump of large, puckered, dark green leaves. Plants grow up to 90 cm (3') tall and spread 45 cm (18"), or more. (Zones 3–8)

Problems and Pests

Generally problem free, horseradish can occasionally suffer from powdery mildew, downy mildew, fungal leaf spot or root rot.

Kale, Collards, Mustard Greens

Brassica

Features: tender biennial; decorative, bronze, purple, blue-green or glossy green, sometimes deeply wrinkled, edible leaves **Height:** 45–60 cm (18–24") **Spread:** 45–60 cm (18–24")

These nutrient-packed, leafy cabbage and broccoli siblings are some of the most decorative members of this family. Collards are not grown as often in Canada as they are in the southern U.S., but they grow quite happily here and make a welcome change from cabbage and kale. Mustards are most often eaten when quite young and lend a spicy flavour to stir-fries and salads.

Starting

All three of these plants can be sown directly into the garden. They are all quite cold hardy and can be planted pretty much as soon as the soil can be worked in spring. A light frost won't harm them, though you may wish to cover the young plants if nighttime temperatures are expected to get to -10° C (14° F), or lower. You may wish to make several successive plantings of mustard because the leaves have the best flavour when they are young and tender.

Growing

These plants grow best in **full sun**. The soil should be **fertile, moist** and **well drained**. Mustard in particular should not be allowed to dry out, or the leaves may develop a bitter flavour.

Harvesting

Once plants are established, you can start harvesting leaves as needed. Pick a few of the outer leaves from each plant.

Tips

Because the leaves are what you will be eating, you don't have to wait very long after planting to start harvesting. These plants make a striking addition to beds and borders where the foliage creates a good compliment and backdrop for plants with brightly coloured flowers.

Recommended

B. oleracea subsp. *acephala* (kale, collards) and *B. juncea* subsp. *rugosa* (mustard) form large clumps of ruffled, creased or wrinkled leaves in shades of green, blue-green, bronze and purple.

'**Blue Curled**' and '**Blue Ridge**' are popular selections of kale. '**Mizouna**' and '**Savanna**' are popular mustard selections. '**Green Glaze**' is a popular selection of collards, often referred to as "greasy greens."

Problems and Pests

Problems with cutworms, leaf miners, caterpillars, root maggots, cabbage white butterfly larvae, white rust, downy mildew and powdery mildew can occur.

Kohlrabi

Brassica

Features: biennial, grown as an annual; pale slivery or grey-green foliage; edible bulbous stem base **Height:** 30 cm (12") **Spread:** 30 cm (12")

The tender, swollen stem base of kohlrabi is curious looking. The leave bases become stretched as the bulb forms, and new leaves continue to sprout from the top of the rounded bulb.

Starting

Seed can be sown directly in the garden around the last frost date. This plant matures quite quickly, so make several small sowings one or two weeks apart to have tender, young kohlrabi for most of summer.

Growing

Kohlrabi grows best in **full sun.** The soil should be **fertile, moist** and **well drained,** though plants adapt to most moist soils.

Harvesting

Keep a close eye on your kohlrabi, because the bulb can become tough and woody quickly if left too long before harvesting. The bulb is generally well rounded and 5–10 cm (2–4") in diameter when ready for harvesting. Pull up the entire plant and cut just below the bulb. Then cut the leaves and stems off and compost them or use them to mulch the bed.

Tips

Low and bushy, with white or purple bulbs, kohlrabi makes an interesting edging plant for beds and borders and can be included in container gardens, particularly those you like to change the plantings in regularly.

Recommended

B. oleracea* subsp. *gongylodes forms a low bushy clump of blue-green foliage. As the plant matures, the stem just above ground level swells and becomes rounded. This is the edible part.

Encourage good growth by keeping the soil moist, and harvest quickly once bulbs form.

Problems and Pests

Problems with cutworms, leaf miners, caterpillars, root maggots, cabbage white butterfly larvae, white rust, downy mildew and powdery mildew can occur.

Leeks

Allium

Features: biennial, often grown as an annual; long, strap-shaped, dark blue-green leaves; narrow, upright growth with arching leaves **Height:** 45–60 cm (18–24") **Spread:** 10–20 cm (4–8")

Leeks can rival most ornamental grasses for garden presence. The plants are strongly upright with stunning dark blue-green leaves that arch from the main stem. Planted in a small group, they are a welcome addition to the border.

Starting

Leeks can be sown directly in the garden, but because they take quite a long time to mature, they can also be started indoors 8 to 10 weeks before you plan to plant them outdoors. Such a long time indoors can encourage lanky growth, so if you don't have supplemental lighting or a very bright window, you may find it better to purchase plants when you are ready to plant them outdoors.

Growing

Leeks grow best in **full sun**. The soil should be **fertile** and **well drained**, but plants adapt to most well-drained soils. Improve less than ideal soil by mixing in compost or adding a layer of compost mulch once you have planted. You can mound mulch, soil or straw up around the base of the plants as summer progresses to encourages tender, white growth low on the plant.

Don't feel you have to harvest all your leeks in fall. Some plants can be left in place to be harvested in spring or even left to flower and go to seed. These perennial plants will return year after year, and new seedlings can be allowed to grow in to replace fading plants.

Harvesting

Leeks can be harvested as soon as they are mature in early autumn, but because they are so hardy, you can just harvest them as you need them until the ground begins to freeze. At that point you should pull up any you want for winter use. They keep for several weeks in the refrigerator if you cut the roots short and wrap the leeks in plastic. For longer storage, they can be frozen. Be sure to double bag them so the onion-like flavour doesn't seep into any other food you have in the freezer.

Tips

Leeks are one of the most ornamental of all the onions. They have bright blue-green leaves that cascade from the central stem. The second year from planting, they develop large, globe-shaped clusters of flowers atop 90 cm (3') stems. Plant them in groups in your beds and borders.

Recommended

A. ampeloprasum subsp. ***porrum***
are upright perennials with blue-
green leaves that cascade from the
central stem. Globe-shaped clusters
of flowers are borne atop a tall stem
the second year from planting.

Problems and Pests

Problems with rot, mildew, smut,
rust, leaf spot, onion flies and
thrips can occur.

Lettuce, Mesclun

Letuca

Features: annual; ruffled leaves in shades of green, red and bronze, sometimes spotted, speckled or streaked and bicoloured **Height:** 15–45 cm (6–18") **Spread:** 15–45 cm (6–18")

Lettuce, with its undulating or rippled edges and variable leaf colours, is an ornamental treasure trove that deserves of a spot in the garden, even if you don't care for salad. Mesclun, whether a spicy or a mild blend, makes a welcome addition to salads and stir-fries, while providing a good ground cover in the garden.

Starting

Lettuce and mesclun can be started directly in the garden around the last frost date. You may wish to be more selective when planting head lettuces so you don't have to thin the plants out as much later, but the seeds of leafy lettuces and mesclun can be scattered across a prepared area and do not have to be planted in rows. If you make several smaller plantings spaced a week or two apart, you won't end up with more plants than you can use maturing at once. For an earlier crop, start a few plants indoors about four weeks before you plan to plant them outdoors.

Growing

Lettuce and mesclun grow well in **full sun** or **light** or **partial shade** in a **sheltered** location. The soil should be **fertile, moist** and **well drained**. Add plenty of compost to improve the soil, and be sure to keep your lettuce moist. Lettuce is very prone to drying out in hot and windy situations, so it is best to plant it where it will get some protection from other plants. Plants under too much stress can quickly bolt and go to seed or simply wilt and die.

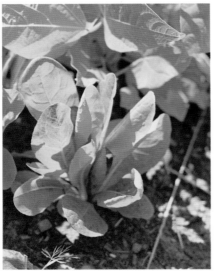

Harvesting

Head-forming lettuce can be harvested once the head is plump. If the weather turns very hot, you may wish to cut heads even earlier because the leaves develop a bitter flavour once plants go to flower. Looseleaf lettuce and mesclun can be harvested by pulling a few leaves off as needed or by cutting an entire plant 5–10 cm (2–4") above ground level. Most will continue to produce new leaves even if cut this way.

Tips

Lettuce and mesclun make interesting additions to container plantings, either alone or combined with other plants. In beds and borders, mesclun makes a decorative edging plant. All lettuces and mesclun are fairly low growing and should be planted near the front of a border so they will be easier to get to for casual picking.

To add a twist to your purchased mesclun mixes, try adding a few herb seeds; cilantro, dill, parsley and basil are a few you may enjoy.

Recommended

L. sativa forms a clump of ruffle-edged leaves and comes in many forms. Loose-leaf lettuce forms a loose rosette of leaves rather than a central head. Butterhead or Boston lettuce forms a loose head and has a very mild flavour. Crisphead or iceberg lettuce forms a very tight head of leaves. Romaine or cos lettuce has a more upright habit, and the heads are fairly loose but cylindrical in shape.

Mesclun mixes can be a combination of different lettuces, usually looseleaf types, eaten while very young and tender. Mixes often also include other species of plants, including mustards, broccoli, radicchio, endive, arugula, chicory and spinach. Most seed catalogues offer a good selection of pre-mixed mesclun as well as separate selections to create your own mix.

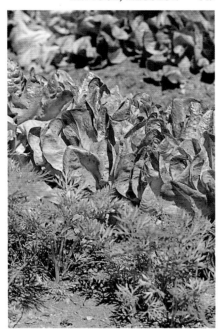

Problems and Pests

Problems with root rot, leaf spot, flea beetle and mosaic virus can occur.

Marigold

Tagetes

Features: annual; edible yellow, red, orange, brown, gold, cream, bicoloured flowers; fragrant foliage **Height:** 15–90 cm (6–36") **Spread:** 15–60 cm (6–24")

From the large, exotic, ruffled flowers of African marigold to the tiny flowers of the low-growing signet marigold, the warm colours and fresh scent of these plants add a festive touch to the garden.

Starting
Marigolds can be sown directly in the garden around the last frost date. Plants can also be purchased from garden centres and nurseries.

Growing
Marigolds grow best in **full sun**. The soil should be of **average fertility** and **well drained**. These plants are drought tolerant but hold up well in windy, rainy weather. Deadhead to prolong blooming and to keep plants tidy.

Harvesting
Flowers should be picked for use once they are fully open. Leaves of signet, lemon mint and Mexican mint marigold can be picked as needed for use in teas, soups and salads.

Tips
Dot these plants in small groups throughout your beds and borders for a pretty display, as well as to take advantage of their reputed nematode-repelling properties. Marigolds also make lovely additions to sunny container plantings.

Recommended
Although *T. erecta* (Aztec marigold, African marigold), *T. patula* (French marigold) and their hybrids have edible flowers, *T. lemmonii* (lemon mint marigold), *T. lucida* (Mexican mint marigold, Mexican mint tarragon) and *T. tenuifolia* (signet marigold) are the most common culinary species.

Problems and Pests
Slugs and snails can ravage the foliage of all marigolds.

Melon

Cucumis

Features: annual; trailing or climbing vine; attractive foliage; yellow flowers
Height: 30 cm (12") **Spread:** 1.5–3 m (5–10')

Success with melons is somewhat limited in most Canadian gardens, because they prefer warmer summer weather and a longer growing season than we can provide them. They are worth trying, though, and in the right spot, they can do really well. As an added bonus, they don't need as much water once the fruit are nearing their mature size, about the same time in late summer that I always start to slack off on my watering.

Starting

Melons can be started indoors about six weeks before you want to transplant them to the garden. They don't like to have their roots disturbed, so plant them in fairly large peat pots so they have plenty of room to grow and can be set directly into the garden once the weather warms up.

Growing

Melons grow best in **full sun** in a warm location. The soil should be **average to fertile, humus rich, moist** and **well drained**. Fruit develops poorly with inconsistent moisture, and plants can rot in cool or soggy soil. Use raised beds or mound soil up before planting to improve drainage. The fruit will be sweeter and more flavourful if you cut back on watering as it is ripening.

If you aren't sure how well melons will grow in your garden, try the shorter season selections, and plant them in the warmest part of the garden.

Harvesting

Melons should be allowed to fully mature on the vine. Muskmelons develop more netting on the rind as they ripen. They generally slip easily from the vine with gentle pressure when ripe. Honeydew melons develop a paler colour when they are ripe. They must be cut from the vine when they are ripe.

Tips

Melons have a well-deserved reputation for spreading, but like most vine-forming plants, they can be trained to grow up rather than out. As the fruit becomes larger, you may need to support it so the vines don't get damaged. You can create hammocks out of old nylon pantyhose to support the melons.

Melons have quite attractive foliage and can also be left to wind through your ornamental beds and borders.

Recommended

C. melo subsp. *reticulatus* (muskmelon) and *C. melo* subsp. *indorus* (honeydew melon) are tender annual vines with attractive green leaves. Bright yellow flowers are produced in summer. Male and female flowers are produced separately on the same vine. The

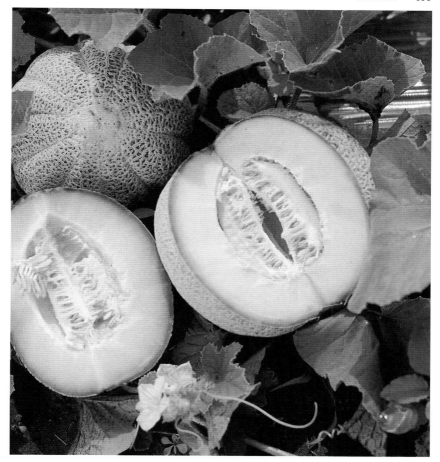

melons are round, green or gold in colour and some, usually muskmelons, develop a corky tan or greenish netting as they ripen. Muskmelons generally develop orange- or salmon-coloured flesh, and honeydew melons develop pale green or yellow-coloured flesh. Most melons take 70–85 days to produce mature, ripe fruit. Popular cultivars include **'Alaska,'** **'Earlidew,'** **'Earlisweet,'** **'Fastbreak,'** **'Gourmet'** and **'Passport.'**

Problems and Pests

Powdery mildew, *fusarium* wilt, cucumber beetles and sap beetles can be quite serious problems. Mildew weakens the plants, and the beetles may introduce wilt, which is fatal to the plants.

When maturity dates are given for vegetables, they usually refer to plants grown in optimum conditions. Cool weather can greatly delay the development of your melons. Choose short-season varieties, but anticipate that you may need a longer season than suggested.

Nasturtium

Tropaeolum

Features: annual; bushy or trailing habits; edible, red, orange, yellow, burgundy, pink, cream, gold, white or bicoloured flowers; attractive, edible foliage **Height:** 30–45 cm (12–18") for dwarf varieties; up to 3 m (10') for trailing varieties **Spread:** equal to height

These fast-growing, brightly coloured flowers are easy to grow, making them popular with beginners and experienced gardeners alike.

T. majus (above)

Starting
Direct sow seed once the danger of frost has passed.

Growing
Nasturtiums prefer **full sun** but tolerate some shade. The soil should be of **poor to average fertility, light, moist** and **well drained**. Soil that is too rich or has too much fertilizer results in a lot of leaves and very few flowers. Let the soil drain completely between waterings.

Harvesting
Pick leaves and flowers for fresh use as needed.

Tips
Nasturtiums are used in beds, borders, containers and hanging baskets and on sloped banks. The climbing varieties are grown up trellises and over rock walls or places that need concealing. These plants thrive in poor locations, and they make interesting additions to plantings on hard-to-mow slopes.

Recommended
T. majus has a trailing habit, but many of the cultivars have bushier, more refined habits. Cultivars offer differing flower colours or variegated foliage.

Problems and Pests
These plants rarely suffer from any problems.

The edible leaves and flowers add a peppery flavour to salads.

Okra

Abelmoschus

Features: bushy annual; attractive foliage, flowers and fruit **Height:** 60 cm–1.2 m (24–48") **Spread:** 60 cm (24")

Okra is another vegetable that is grown with variable success in Canada. Some gardeners have great success, while others are often disappointed. Our seasons can be just a bit too short and our weather not quite hot enough to produce mature okra. When you plant okra, you are hedging your bets on having a hot summer.

Starting

Okra germinates quickly in warm soil. Seeds should be soaked overnight before planting. Start them in peat pots six to eight weeks before you plan to move them to the garden. Wait until the last frost date has passed and the soil has warmed before moving them outside.

Growing

Okra grows best in **full sun** in a **warm, sheltered** location. The soil should be **fertile, moist** and **well drained**.

Harvesting

This plant can be spiny, so it is best to wear gloves when harvesting the fruit. The fruit is picked when still immature, usually a week or two after the flower drops and the pod sets. Pods are usually harvested when they are about 8–10 cm (3–4") long.

Tips

Okra likes hot growing conditions, so include it in the hottest part of your garden, and use plenty of mulch to conserve water. This plant makes an attractive addition to container plantings, with the added bonus that you can extend your growing season by bringing the entire container indoors when cool weather or frost is expected.

Recommended

A. esculentus is a bushy, upright plant with sometimes spiny foliage and brown- or purple-spotted, yellow, hibiscus-like flowers. Flowers are borne at the base of each leaf where it attaches to the stem. Plants mature in about 50 days after being transplanted, but

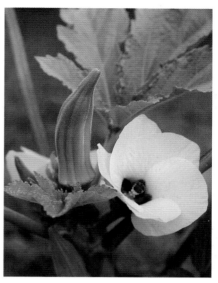

require plenty of hot weather to flower and fruit. **'Burgundy,' 'Cajun Delight'** and **'Dwarf Green'** are a few of the varieties available from Canadian seed suppliers.

Problems and Pests

Occasional problems with slugs, spider mites, whiteflies, cabbage white butterfly larvae, fungal leaf spot or powdery mildew can occur.

A. esculentus 'Cajun Delight' (below)

Onion

Allium

Features: biennial or perennial; upright, tubular green leaves; globe-like flower clusters **Height:** 45–60 cm (18–24") **Spread:** 5–10 cm (2–4")

Onions are one of the oldest cultivated plants, having been grown for over 5000 years. They have been cultivated for so long that their country of origin is not even known.
Grow onions and become a part of history.

Starting

Onions can be started from seed indoors about six to eight weeks before you plan to plant them outdoors; they can also be sown directly in the garden once the last frost date has passed. Sets of starter onions can be purchased and planted in spring. Bunching onions are usually started from seed, sown directly in the garden. They are quick to mature, so make several smaller sowings two or three weeks apart from spring to mid-summer for a regular supply.

Growing

Onions should be grown in **full sun**. The soil should be **fertile, moist** and **well drained**. Onions use plenty of water but will rot in very wet soil. They are poor at competing with other plants, so keep them well weeded. A good layer of mulch will conserve moisture and keep the weeds down. Be sure to water during periods of extended drought.

Harvesting

All onions can be harvested and used as needed throughout the season. Pull up onions that need thinning, and just pinch back the tops if you want the bulbs to mature or the plant to continue to produce leaves.

Bulb onions grown for storage are ready to be harvested when the leaves begin to yellow and flop over and the shoulders of the bulbs are just visible above the soil line. They should be pulled up and allowed to dry for a few days before being stored in a dry, cold, frost-free spot.

Onions are perennials and can also be left in the ground over winter, though the flavour can become quite strong the second year. They will flower the second summer.

Tips

Onions have fascinating cylindrical leaves that add an interesting vertical accent to the garden. Include them in beds and borders, but if you want big bulbs, don't let them be overly crowded by other plants. Smaller bulbs form on plants that are too crowded, not a bad idea if you only want small bulbs.

Onions also make interesting additions to container plantings, particularly close to the house, if you just want to pick a few leaves at a time.

A. fistulosum (above)

Recommended

A. cepa (bulb onion) forms a clump of cylindrical foliage and develops a large, round or flattened bulb. Bulb formation is day-length dependant. Canadian gardeners tend to use northern onion varieties that have been developed for long days. Bulb formation begins when days are 15–16 hours long.

A. fistulosum (bunching onion, green onion, shallots) is a perennial that forms a clump of foliage. The plant quickly begins to divide and multiply from the base. Plants may develop small bulbs or no bulbs at all. Once established, these plants will provide you with green onions all spring and summer.

Problems and Pests

Problems with smut, onion maggots and rot can occur.

A. fistulosum (above)

Oregano · Marjoram

Origanum

Features: fragrant foliage; white or pink summer flowers **Height:** 30–80 cm (12–32")
Spread: 20–45 cm (8–18")

Oregano and marjoram are two of the best-known and most frequently used herbs. They are popular in stuffings, soups and stews, and no pizza is complete until it has been sprinkled with fresh or dried oregano.

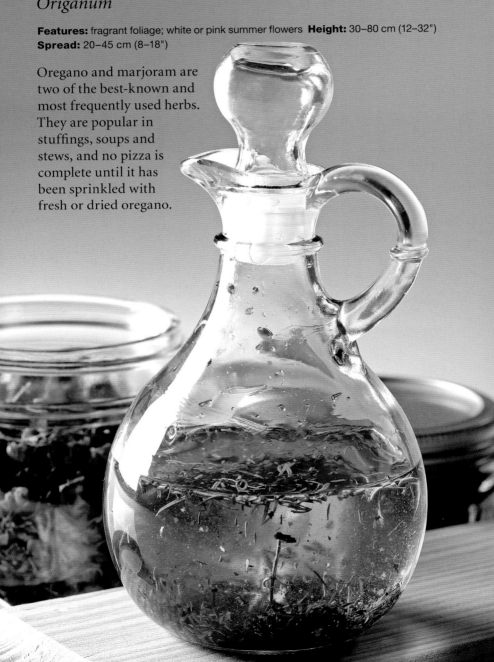

Starting

These plants can be started from seed four to six weeks before you plan to plant them into the garden. You can also purchase plants, but use a reputable source so you can be sure you purchase the exact variety you want.

Growing

Oregano and marjoram grow best in **full sun**. The soil should be **average to fertile, neutral to alkaline** and **well drained**. The flowers attract pollinators and beneficial insects to the garden. Oregano may self-seed.

Harvesting

Leaves can be picked as needed for fresh use or dried for use in winter.

Tips

These bushy perennials make lovely additions to any border and can be trimmed to form low hedges.

Recommended

O. majorana (marjoram) is upright and shrubby. It has hairy, light green leaves and bears white or pink flowers in summer. Where it is not hardy, it can be grown as an annual. (Zones 5–9)

O. vulgare var. *hirtum* (oregano, Greek oregano) is the most flavourful culinary variety of oregano. This low, bushy plant has hairy, grey-green leaves and bears white flowers. Many other interesting varieties of *O. vulgare* are available, including those with golden, variegated or curly leaves. (Zones 5–9)

Problems and Pests

Problems with oregano and marjoram are rare.

Oriental Cabbage

Brassica

Features: annual; upright, leafy plants **Height:** 45 cm (18") **Spread:** 30 cm (12")

A tasty ingredient in stir-fries and soups, Oriental cabbage is also an interesting addition to the garden. It has light or dark green, white-veined leaves with undulating or ruffled edges.

Starting

Start seeds indoors four to six weeks before the last frost date. Transplant young plants outdoors once the last frost date has passed and the soil has warmed up.

Growing

Oriental cabbage grows best in **full sun**. The soil should be **fertile, moist** and **well drained**. Mulch to keep the soil moist. Oriental cabbage is more tolerant of warm, humid weather than some of the other members of the *Brassica* family, making it a useful addition to hotter Canadian gardens.

Harvesting

Oriental cabbage comes in two basic forms; solid heads that are cut whole and looser heads with leaves that can be removed as needed.

Tips

This cabbage can be grown in containers where it can be combined with other edible or flowering plants. Dotted through a border, it creates a low but upright feature, adding its unique colour and form.

Recommended

B. rapa* subsp. *chinensis (pac choi, bok choi) forms a loose clump of blue-green leaves with thick, fleshy, white or light green stems.

B. rapa* subsp. *pekinensis (Chinese cabbage) forms a dense head of tightly packed leaves.

Problems and Pests

Cutworms, leaf miners, caterpillars, root maggots, cabbage white butterfly larvae, white rust, downy mildew and powdery mildew can be problematic.

Many seed catalogues offer a selection of Oriental vegetables. Some of them are cultivars or species of plants we recognize, while others are unique. Try a few to expand your vegetable repertoire.

Parsley

Petroselinum

Features: biennial, grown as an annual; attractive foliage; bushy habit
Height: 20–60 cm (8–24") **Spread:** 30–60 cm (12–24")

Although often used just as a garnish, parsley is rich in vitamins and minerals and is reputed to freshen the breath after garlic or onion-rich foods are eaten.

Starting

Parsley can be sown directly in the garden once the last frost date has passed or four to six weeks earlier indoors. Start it in peat pots or in its permanent location, because parsley resents having its roots disturbed.

Growing

Parsley grows well in **full sun** or **partial shade**. The soil should be **average to fertile, humus rich, moist** and **well drained**.

Harvesting

Pinch parsley back to encourage bushy growth, and use the sprigs you pick off for eating. This plant can also be cut back regularly if you need a larger quantity in a recipe, and if not cut back too hard, it will sprout new growth.

Tips

Containers of parsley can be kept close to the house for easy picking. The bright green leaves and compact habit make parsley a good edging plant for beds and borders.

Recommended

P. crispum forms a clump of bright green, divided leaves. This biennial is usually grown as an annual because it is the leaves that are desired and not the flowers or seeds. Cultivars may have flat or curly leaves. Flat leaves are tastier and curly ones more decorative. Dwarf cultivars are also available.

Problems and Pests

Parsley rarely suffers from any problems.

Parsnip

Pastinaca

Features: biennial, grown as an annual; sweet, edible root; feathery foliage **Height:** 30–45 cm (12–18") **Spread:** 15–20 cm (6–8")

Despite needing a fairly long season to mature, parsnip is well suited to northern gardens because it is best eaten once it has had a few goods frosts to sweeten its roots.

Starting

Sow seed directly into the garden as soon as the soil can be worked. Be sure to keep the soil moist to ensure good germination. Seed can be slow to germinate, sometimes taking up to three weeks, so mark the location where you plant it.

Growing

Parsnip grows best in **full sun** but tolerates some light shade. The soil should be of **average fertility, moist** and **well drained**. Be sure to work the soil well and mix in compost to improve the texture. Roots develop poorly in heavy soil. Mulch to suppress weed growth and to conserve moisture.

Harvesting

The roots can be pulled up in autumn, after the first few frosts, and stored, like carrots, in damp sand in a cold, frost-free location. This plant can also be mulched with straw and pulled up in spring, before it sprouts new growth. Frost improves the flavour because some of the root starches are converted to sugar in freezing weather.

Tips

Not the most ornamental of vegetables, parsnip provides a nice, dark, leafy background to lower-growing plants and produces plenty of vegetables for very little effort.

Recommended

P. sativa is an upright plant with dark green divided leaves. It develops a long, pale creamy yellow root that looks like a carrot. **'Andover,' 'Harris Model'** and **'Hollow Crown'** are commonly available cultivars.

P. sativa

Problems and Pests

Canker, carrot rust fly and onion maggot can affect parsnip.

Roasting the roots brings out their sweetness. Combine parsnips with potatoes, carrots and other root vegetables, then drizzle with oil and sprinkle with herbs before roasting for an hour, or until the vegetables are tender.

Peas

Pisum

Features: climbing annual; bright green foliage; white flowers
Height: 30 cm–1.5 m (1–5') **Spread:** 10–20 cm (4–8")

Some of my favourite childhood memories involve the growing, shelling and eating of peas. My sister and I particularly enjoyed counting the peas in the pod to see what the greatest number would be. I seem to recall 14 or 16 being the most we ever counted in a single pod.

Starting

Peas show an admirable appreciation for cool spring weather and can be planted directly outdoors as soon as the soil can be worked and has dried out a bit. A light frost or two won't do them any harm, but the seeds can rot in cold, wet soil. And the sooner they are planted, the sooner you can begin eating peas. Peas, like beans, can be treated with bacterial inoculant before planting to ensure a good supply of nitrogen-fixing bacteria on the roots.

Growing

Peas grow well in **full sun**. The soil should be **average to fertile, humus rich, moist** and **well drained**. Peas can grow a wide range of heights, but all benefit from a support of some kind to grow up. They develop small tendrils that twine around twiggy branches, nets or chain-link fences. Base your support height on the expected height of the plants, and make sure it is in place before your seeds sprout because the roots are quite shallow and can be damaged quite easily.

Harvesting

Peas should be harvested when they are still young and tender. They can be pulled from the vine by hand, but use both hands, one to hold the plant and one to pull the pea pod, to avoid damaging the plant. The more you pick, the more peas the plants will produce.

Tips

Peas are excellent plants for growing up a low chain-link fence, and the taller varieties create a privacy screen quite quickly. The low-growing and medium-height peas make interesting additions to hanging baskets and container plantings. They can grow up the hangers or supports or can be encouraged to spill over the edges and trail down.

Recommended

P. sativum var. *sativum* are climbing plants with bright green, waxy stems and leaves and white flowers. The resulting pods are grouped into three categories: shelling peas, snow peas and snap peas. The seeds are removed from the pods of shelling peas and are the only part eaten. Snow peas are eaten as flat, seedless pods. Snap peas develop fat seeds, and the pod and seeds are eaten together.

There are many peas to choose from. When deciding which to grow, think about the type of peas you will get the most use from. Then choose the mature plant height that is most suitable for the space you have.

Problems and Pests

Peas are somewhat prone to powdery mildew, so choose mildew-resistant varieties and avoid touching the plants when they are wet to prevent the spread of disease. Aphids and whiteflies can also cause problems.

Peppers, Chiles
Capiscum

Features: bushy annual; attractive foliage; white flowers; colourful fruit
Height: 15–60 cm (6–24") **Spread:** 30–45 cm (12–18")

The variety of sweet and chili peppers is nothing short of remarkable. Among the many different shapes, colours and flavours of peppers, there is sure to be one or two that appeal. A cool summer can really put a damper on fruiting, which can make hot pepper growing, in particular, a bit tricky in Canadian gardens.

Starting

Peppers need warmth to germinate and grow, and they take a while to mature, so it is best to start them indoors 6–10 weeks before the last frost date. If you don't have ideal light conditions, your seedlings may become stretched out and do poorly even when moved to the garden. In this case, you may prefer to purchase started plants; many varieties are available at garden centres and nurseries.

Growing

Peppers grow best in **full sun** in a warm location. The soil should be **average to fertile, moist** and **well drained**. Mulch to ensure the soil stays moist, because most Canadians need to plant their peppers in a fairly hot garden location. Most gardens will be hot enough to grow sweet peppers, but chili peppers need hotter weather to bear fruit. Try a dark mulch in a hot spot if you've had little luck with these peppers in the past.

Harvesting

Peppers can be picked as needed, once they are ripe. Chili peppers can also be dried for use in winter.

Tips

Pepper plants are neat and bushy. Once the peppers set and begin to ripen, the plants can be very colourful as the bright red, orange and yellow fruit contrasts beautifully with the dark green of the foliage. They are a worthwhile addition to a hot and sunny border, even if you don't care to eat peppers. All peppers are good additions to container plantings. Chili peppers in particular are useful in containers because they usually have the most interesting fruit shapes, and the containers can be moved indoors or to a sheltered spot to extend the season if needed. Some of the smaller chili peppers also make interesting houseplants for warm, sunny windows.

Capsaicin is the chemical that gives peppers their heat. Peppers may be rated on a scale of 1–10 or by Scoville units. Sweet peppers have about 100 Scoville units while habaneros can have up to 350,000 Scoville units.

Recommended

C. annuum is the most common species of sweet and hot peppers. Plants are bushy with dark green foliage. Flowers are white, and peppers can be shades of green, red, orange, yellow, purple or brown. Cultivars of sweet peppers include **'Blushing Beauty,' 'Carmen,' 'Earlibird'** and **'Orange Sun.'** Cultivars of chili peppers include **'Anaheim,' 'Cayenne,' 'Jalapeno,' 'Scotch Bonnet'** and **'Thai,'** just to name a few.

C. chinense **'Habanero'** is one of the hottest of the chili peppers. It is native to the Caribbean.

Problems and Pests

Rare problems with aphids and whiteflies can occur.

C. annuum (above)

Poppy
Papaver

Features: red, pink, white or purple, single or double flowers; edible seeds
Height: 30 cm–1.2 m (1–4') **Spread:** 20–45 cm (8–18")

Poppy seeds are a frequent addition to baked goods. Remarkably easy to grow, poppies also add abundant colour to your garden.

P. somniferum (photos this page)

Starting

Direct sow poppies in spring. Several smaller sowings will give you a longer flower display, but this isn't necessary if you are just growing poppies for the seeds. The seeds are very small, and you will get better distribution if you mix them with fine sand before you plant them. Because they need light to germinate, the seeds shouldn't be covered when you plant them.

Growing

Poppies grow best in **full sun**. The soil should be **fertile, sandy, humus rich** and **well drained**. Good drainage is essential.

Harvesting

You will know the seeds are ready to be harvested when the pods begin to dry and you can hear the seeds rattle in the pods when you shake them gently. Cut the heads off and shake the seeds into a paper bag. Let them dry in the paper bag and then store them in a jar or other container.

Tips

Poppies work well in mixed borders where other plants are slow to fill in. Poppies will fill empty spaces early in the season, then die back over summer, leaving room for other plants.

They also self-seed freely and are likely to continue to spring up in your garden once you've planted them.

Recommended

P. somniferum (opium poppy) forms a basal rosette of foliage above which leafy stems bear red, pink, white or purple flowers. Large blue-green seedpods follow the flowers. Propagation of the species is restricted in many countries because of its narcotic properties. Several acceptable cultivars are available for ornamental and culinary purposes. Blue-, white- or brown-seeded varieties are available.

Problems and Pests

Poppies rarely suffer from any problems.

You might want to keep your poppies in the back garden. Law enforcement officials have been known to insist people remove their poppies despite the culinary varieties having little or none of the narcotic properties that makes the species illegal.

Potatoes

Solanum

Features: bushy annual; leafy, rounded habit; pink, purple or white flowers
Height: 45–60 cm (18–24") **Spread:** 30–60 cm (12–24")

Potatoes were cultivated in South America for centuries and were introduced to Europe by the Spanish. They were only introduced to North America after European immigrants brought them here.

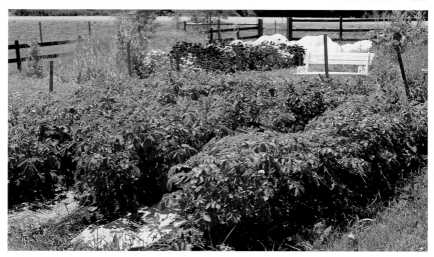

Starting

Sets of seed potatoes (small tubers) can be purchased and planted in spring a few weeks before the last frost date, as long as the soil isn't cold and wet. Young plants can tolerate a light frost, but not a hard freeze. The seed potatoes can be cut into smaller pieces, as long as each has an "eye," the dimpled spot from which the plant and roots grow. Each piece needs 30–45 cm (12–18") of space to grow.

Growing

Potatoes prefer **full sun** but tolerate some shade. The soil should be **fertile, humus rich, acidic, moist** and **well drained,** though potatoes adapt to most growing conditions and tolerate both hot and cold weather. Mound soil up around the plants to keep the tubers out of the light as they develop.

All parts of the potato plant are poisonous except the tubers, and they can become poisonous if they are exposed to light. Green flesh is a good indication that your potatoes have been exposed to light. To protect your potatoes, mound soil around the plants, 2.5 cm (1") or so per week, from mid-summer to fall. A straw mulch also effectively shades the developing tubers.

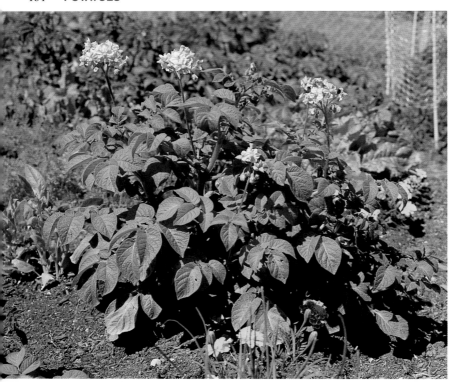

Harvesting

The tubers begin to form around the same time the plants begin to flower, usually some time in August. You can dig up a few tubers at a time from this point on as you need them. The remaining crop should be dug up in autumn once the plants have withered, but before the first hard frost. Let them dry for a few hours on the soil, and then brush the dirt off and store the tubers in a cold, dark place. You can even save a few of the smaller tubers for planting the following spring.

Tips

These large, bushy plants with white, pink or light purple flowers are good filler plants for an immature border and are excellent at breaking up the soil in newer gardens.

Recommended

S. tuberosum is a bushy, mound-forming plant. It bears tiny, exotic-looking, white, pink or light purple flowers in late summer. There are many varieties of potatoes available. They can have rough or smooth, white, yellow, brown, red or blue skin and white, yellow, purple or blue flesh. A few popular varieties include **'All-Blue,'** with smooth blue skin and light purple-blue flesh; **'Irish Cobbler,'** with smooth brown skin and white flesh; **'Norland,'** with smooth red skin and white flesh; and **'Yukon Gold,'** with smooth light beige skin and yellow flesh.

Problems and Pests

Potatoes are susceptible to a variety of diseases, including scab. Avoid planting them in the same spot two years in a row. Potato beetle is the most troublesome insect pest.

Purchase seed sets of a variety that interests you rather than trying to grow potatoes bought from the grocery store. They may have been treated to prevent sprouting, or they may be poorly suited to grow where you live.

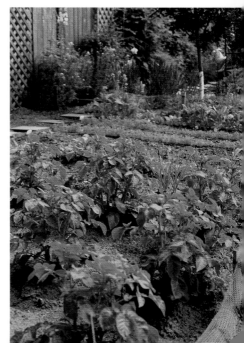

Quinoa

Chenopodium

Features: branching, upright annual; soft leaves; attractive flowerheads; good fall colour **Height:** 1.5–2.4 m (5–8') **Spread:** 30–45 cm (12–18")

Quinoa is another protein-rich, easy-to-grow, nutty flavoured grain that looks great in the garden. The colourful seedheads form in clusters at the tips of the branches.

Starting

Sow directly in the garden once the soil has dried out a bit and can be worked. Young plants tolerate a light frost. Seeds can be scattered over an area or planted in rows. Keep the seedbed moist during germination. Young seedlings resemble the weed lamb's quarters, so take care when weeding not to pull up the plants you want.

Growing

Quinoa grows best in **full sun**. The soil should be **average to fertile** and **well drained,** though the plant adapts to most conditions and is drought tolerant once established. A layer of mulch will conserve moisture and keep weeds down, though this plant's leafy habit tends to suppress weed growth once the plant starts to fill in. Quinoa is a good choice for Canadian gardens; it grows well in our climate and enjoys our summer temperatures.

Harvesting

The seeds generally ripen around the time of the first autumn frost. The leaves die back around the same time, making harvesting a simple matter of grasping the stem with a gloved hand and pulling upwards to remove the seeds. Remove plant bits by running your hands through the collected seeds on a lightly breezy day or by blowing a fan across the surface to blow away the dry plant bits. Seeds should be dried completely before storing.

Quinoa seeds are coated in a bitter substance called saponin. Lighter coloured seeds have less saponin. Rinse the seeds vigorously in water to wash the saponin off. The water will cease to foam when the saponin is gone. You can even put the seeds in a pillowcase or mesh bag and run them through a cycle in the washing machine (without soap) to rinse large quantities thoroughly.

Tips

This lovely, tall plant, with its seed-heads that ripen to shades of gold, orange and red, is a welcome addition to the autumn garden. Combine it with other tall autumn bloomers, such as sunflowers and amaranth, to create a stunning display along a fence or wall.

Recommended

C. quinoa is a tall, leafy, branching annual plant. Flowers are borne in dense clusters along the tips of the stems. The leaves turn shades of orange and red in autumn, and the seeds ripen to shades of red, orange, gold, green or pink. Seeds may be brown, yellow or white. There are many cultivars, though they can be a bit difficult to find. **'Isluga'** has yellow-gold or pink seedheads that produce plenty of yellow seeds. **'Multi-hued'** bears flowers in shades of red, orange and purple. **'Temuco'** has chartreuse and red seedheads and white seeds.

Problems and Pests

Leaves are eaten by a few insects and are susceptible to a few diseases, but seed production is rarely affected.

Your plants should be 30–45 cm (12–18″) apart. If they are filling in too densely, thin out the extra seedlings and add them to salads, or steam them and serve them like spinach. Young leaves can also be prepared this way.

Radish
Daikon Radish
Raphanus

Features: annual; rosette of foliage; fast growing **Height:** 15–20 cm (6–8")
Spread: 10–15 cm (4–6")

Radishes are grouped into two categories. Spring or salad radishes, which include the familiar round, red radishes and the icicle radishes, are used in salads. Winter radishes, which include Oriental or daikon radishes and Spanish radishes, are eaten raw or cooked and can be pickled. The spicy pods of some Oriental radishes are also popular in salads.

Starting

Direct sow seed in spring, as soon as the soil warms up a bit and can be worked. Plants tolerate light frost. Successive, smaller plantings can be made every couple of weeks to ensure a steady supply of radishes. Daikon and other radishes that can be stored for winter can also be started in mid-summer to be harvested in autumn.

Growing

Radishes grow well in **full sun** or **light shade**. The soil should be of **average fertility, loose, humus rich, moist** and **well drained**. Heavy or rocky soils cause the roots to be rough, woody and unpleasant tasting.

Harvesting

Spring radishes should be picked and eaten as soon as the roots develop. The flavour and texture deteriorates quickly if they are left in the ground or stored for too long.

Daikon and Spanish radishes are usually started in summer to be ready for harvest in late autumn. They can be stored like carrots, in moist sand in a cool, dry location. They can also be pickled.

Radishes tend to bolt in hot weather, and the roots develop an unpleasantly hot flavour. Choose icicle types for your summer growing, because they are more tolerant of hot weather than the round, red varieties.

Tips

Easy to grow and a great addition to salads, radishes are also great nurse plants. If planted with mature plants or those that are small-seeded or slow to germinate, such as parsnips and carrots, radishes will shade out weeds and reduce evaporation. Radishes sprout and mature quickly; some varieties are ready to harvest within a month.

Because of their leafy, low-growing habit, these plants make interesting edging plants for borders and are unique additions to container plantings. Use radishes for a quick-growing spring display that will be replaced by other plants once the weather warms up.

Recommended

R. sativus forms a low clump of leaves. The edible roots can be long and slender or short and round; the skin can be rosy red, white or black.

Problems and Pests

Flea beetles and cabbage maggots are common problems for radishes.

Radishes are related to cabbage, broccoli and mustard.

Cabbage maggots on radishes (right)

Raspberries & Blackberries

Rubus

Features: thicket-forming shrubs; long, arching canes; spring flowers; summer fruit
Height: 90 cm–3 m (3–10') **Spread:** 1.2–1.5 m (4–5'), or more

The sweet, juicy berries of these shrubs are popular for use in pies, jams and other fruity desserts, but they are just as delicious when eaten fresh. Thickets are often pruned and staked to form neat rows but can be left to spread freely if you have the space.

Starting

Bare root canes should be purchased in late winter or early spring and should be planted while they are still dormant. Container-grown plants are often available all season, but they may not establish as well.

Growing

Raspberries and blackberries grow well in **full sun, light shade** or **partial shade,** though the best fruiting occurs in full sun. The soil should be of **average fertility, humus rich, moist** and **well drained**. These plants prefer a location **sheltered** from strong winds. Blackberries, in particular, are prone to winter damage. Prune out some of the older canes each year once plants become established to keep plants vigorous and to control their spread.

Blackberries have very long, flexible canes. They can stand freely without staking, but they may take up less room if they are loosely tied to a supportive structure such as a stout post or fence.

If you have more fruit than you can use, spread the excess out on a paper-lined cookie sheet and freeze it. Transfer the fruit to a plastic bag once it is frozen.

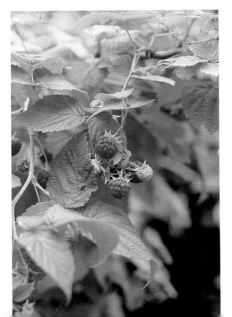

Harvesting

Pick fruit as soon as it is ripe in mid- to late summer. All the fruit does not ripen at once, and you can harvest it for a month or more. Some raspberry varieties are ever-bearing and produce fruit in flushes from mid-summer through autumn.

Tips

These shrubs form rather formidable thickets and can be used in shrub and mixed borders, along fences and as hedges.

Recommended

R. fruticosus (blackberries, brambles) forms a thicket of thorny stems or canes. Canes can grow up to 3 m (10') long, and thickets can spread 1.5 m (5'), or more. White, or occasionally pink, late spring or early summer flowers are followed by red or black berries in late summer. Thornless varieties are also available. (Zones 5–8)

R. idaeus (raspberries) forms a thicket of bristly stems or canes. Canes grow 90 cm–1.5 m (3–5'), and thickets can spread to 1.2 m (4'), or more. White spring flowers are followed by red, yellow, black or purple fruit in mid-summer. Raspberries fall into two categories: summer-bearing and ever-bearing. Although raspberry shrubs are perennial, the canes are biennial, generally growing the first year and producing fruit the second. In the third season, the canes die back. Ever-bearing canes begin to fruit late in the season of their first autumn, then again the second summer. They are suitable in regions where autumn is long and warm; summer-bearing varieties are more suitable for shorter season areas. (Zones 3–8)

Problems and Pests
Problems with anthracnose, powdery mildew, rust, fire blight, leafhoppers and caterpillars can occur.

Rhubarb

Rheum

Features: clump-forming perennial; red or green stems; large, deeply veined leaves; spikes of flowers in summer **Height:** 60 cm–1.2 m (2–4') **Spread:** 90 cm–1.8 m (3–6')

Like tomatoes, rhubarb treads the fine line between fruit and vegetable. We usually eat it in fruit dishes and think of it more as a fruit, but rhubarb is actually a vegetable.

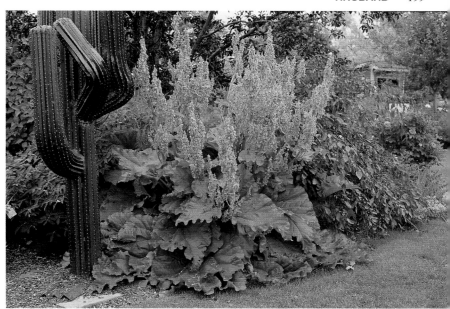

Starting

Rhubarb can be started from seed sown directly in the garden, or crowns can be purchased in spring. If you've planted crowns, you can begin harvesting the second summer. Seeded plants may take three or more years before they produce harvestable vegetables. If friends or neighbours have a rhubarb plant, ask them if they will give you a division from their plant.

Growing

Rhubarb grows best in **full sun**. The soil should be **fertile, humus rich, moist** and **well drained,** but this plant adapts to most conditions. Gently work some compost into the soil around the rhubarb each year, and add a layer of compost mulch. A fertile soil encourages more and bigger stems. Rhubarb can stay in one spot for many years but will remain more vigorous and productive

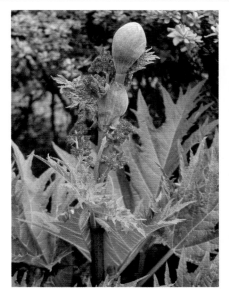

if divided every eight or so years. Dig the soil over and work some more compost in when you divide the plant. Roots can be broken into smaller sections; each piece will sprout as long as it has an "eye."

Inedible ornamental rhubarb (below)

Harvesting

Harvest the stems by pulling them firmly and cleanly from the base of the plant. The leaves can then be cut from the stems with a sharp knife and composted or spread around the base of the plant to conserve moisture, suppress weed growth and return nutrients to the soil. Don't remove more than half the stems from the plant in one year. Rhubarb's flavour is better earlier in summer, and harvesting generally stops by early July when the stems start to become dry, pithy and bitter.

Tips

Sadly, this stunning plant is often relegated to back corners and waste areas in the garden. With its dramatic leaves, bright red stems and intriguing flowers, rhubarb deserves a far more central location.

Recommended
R. rhabarbarum and **R. x hybridum** form large clumps of glossy, deeply veined, green, bronzy or reddish leaves. The edible stems can be green, red or a bit of both. Spikes of densely clustered red, yellow or green flowers are produced in midsummer. Popular varieties include **'Colossal,'** with huge leaves and stems, **'Crimson Cherry'** and **'Victoria.'** (Zones 2–8)

Problems and Pests
Rhubarb rarely suffers from any problems.

Only the stems of rhubarb are edible. The leaves contain oxalic acid in toxic quantities.

Although the flowers are quite interesting and attractive, they are often removed to prolong the stem harvest.

Rosemary

Rosemarinus

Features: fragrant, evergreen foliage; bright blue, sometimes pink flowers
Height: 20 cm–1.2 m (8–48")
Spread: 30 cm–1.2 m (12–48")

The needle-like leaves of this fragrant little shrub are used to flavour a wide variety of foods, including chicken, pork, lamb, rice, tomato and egg dishes.

To overwinter a container-grown plant, keep it in very light or partial shade outdoors in summer, then put it in a sunny window indoors for winter and keep it well watered, allowing it to dry out slightly between waterings.

Starting
Specific varieties of this plant can be purchased from garden centres, nurseries and specialty growers. Seed for the species is available but usually not for specific varieties. It can be started indoors in late winter.

Growing
Rosemary prefers **full sun** but tolerates partial shade. The soil should be of **poor to average fertility** and **well drained**. This tender shrub must be moved indoors for winter.

Harvesting
Leaves can be picked as needed for use in cooking.

Tips
Rosemary is often grown in a shrub border where hardy. In Canada, where it is only hardy in a few places, it is usually grown in a container as a specimen or with other plants. A low-growing, spreading plant can be included in a rock garden or along the top of a retaining wall, or it can be grown in a hanging basket.

Recommended
R. officinalis is a dense, bushy, evergreen shrub with narrow, dark green leaves. The habit varies somewhat between cultivars, from strongly upright to prostrate and spreading. Flowers are usually shades of blue, but pink-flowered cultivars are available. Cultivars that are hardy in a sheltered spot in zone 6 with winter protection are also available. Plants rarely reach their mature size when grown in containers. (Zone 8)

Problems and Pests
Aphids and whiteflies can be a problem on plants overwintering indoors.

Rutabaga

Brassica

Features: rosette-forming biennial; edible roots; blue-green foliage
Height: 30–60 cm (12–24") **Spread:** 10–20 cm (4–8")

One of the tastiest of the root vegetables, rutabaga is not as popular as it deserves to be. I suspect that, as with many maligned vegetables, poor preparation methods are to blame. Try it in soups and stews, where it adds a warm, buttery, sweet flavour.

Starting
Sow seeds directly into the garden in spring. Keep the seedbed moist until the plant germinates.

Growing
Rutabaga prefers to grow in **full sun**. The soil should be **fertile, moist** and **well drained**. The roots can develop discoloured centres in boron-deficient soil. Work agricultural boron into the soil if needed.

Harvesting
Rutabaga is harvested in autumn and stored for winter use. It can be used as soon as the root is plump and round, but can also be left in the ground so the first few autumn frosts can sweeten the roots. Dig it up, cut the greens off and let it dry just enough so the dirt can be brushed off, then store it in moist sand in a cold, frost-free location for winter.

Tips
Rutabaga grows large, bushy clumps of blue-green foliage and can be included in the middle of the border where, though it isn't particularly showy, it provides an attractive, contrasting background for other plants.

Recommended
B. napus (rutabaga, swede, winter turnip) forms a large clump of blue-green leaves. The leaves are not edible. The roots are most often white with purple tops and have yellow flesh. A few varieties are usually available. **'Laurentian'** and its many variations are commonly available and are popular because they store well. Choose a variation

that is clubroot resistant, if this disease is common in your region. **'York'** is good for storing and is clubroot resistant.

Problems and Pests
Cabbage root maggots, cabbage worms, aphids, flea beetles, rust, fungal diseases, downy mildew, powdery mildew and clubroot are possible problems.

The rutabaga originated in Europe and has been in cultivation for over 4000 years.

Sage
Salvia

Features: fragrant, decorative foliage; blue or purple summer flowers
Height: 30–60 cm (12–24") **Spread:** 45–90 cm (18–36")

Sage is perhaps best known as a flavouring for stuffings, but it has a great range of uses, including in soups, stews, sausages and dumplings.

Starting

Specific varieties of sage can be purchased, and the species can be started indoors in late winter or early spring.

Growing

Sage prefers **full sun** but tolerates light shade. The soil should be of **average fertility** and **well drained**. This plant benefits from a light mulch of compost each year. It is drought tolerant once established.

Harvesting

Pick leaves as you need them for fresh use. They can be dried or frozen in late summer and autumn for winter use. A winter mulch of straw often provides enough protection for sage to survive up to a zone 3 winter.

Tips

Sage is a good plant for the border, adding volume to the middle or as an attractive edging or feature plant near the front. Sage can also be grown in mixed planters.

Recommended

S. officinalis is a woody, mound-forming perennial with soft, grey-green leaves. Spikes of light purple or blue flowers appear in early and mid-summer. Many cultivars with attractive foliage are available, including the silver-leaved **'Berggarten,'** the yellow-margined **'Icterina,'** the purple-leaved **'Purpurea,'** and the purple, green and cream variegated **'Tricolor,'** which also has a pink flush to the new growth.

Problems and Pests

Sage rarely suffers from any problems, but it can rot in wet soil.

Sorrel

Rumex

Features: low-growing perennial; tangy, edible leaves **Height:** 15–90 cm (6–36")
Spread: 60 cm (24")

Sorrel can be classified somewhere between a salad green and an herb.
The tangy, sour leaves are a perfect addition to a salad of mixed
greens, but the leaves can also be used to add flavour to soups,
marinades and egg dishes.

*Oxalic acid gives sorrel leaves their
flavour, and though they are safe to
eat, in large quantities they can cause
stomach upset.*

R. acetosa

Starting

Sow the seed directly in the garden in autumn or spring. You can start the seed early indoors, but it isn't really necessary because it grows quickly.

Growing

Sorrel grows well in **full sun** or **light** or **partial shade**, especially in hotter parts of Canada. The soil should be **average to fertile, acidic, humus rich, moist** and **fairly well drained,** but this plant is fairly adaptable. Mulch to conserve moisture. Divide sorrel every three or four years to keep the plant vigorous and the leaves tender and tasty. This plant self-seeds if flowering spikes are not removed.

Harvesting

Pick leaves as needed in spring and early summer. Remove flower spikes as they emerge to prolong the leaf harvest. Once the weather warms up and the plant goes to flower, the leaves lose their pleasant flavour. If you cut the plant back a bit at this point, you will have fresh leaves to harvest in late summer and autumn when the weather cools again.

Tips

A tasty and decorative addition to the vegetable, herb or ornamental garden, French sorrel also makes an attractive groundcover and can be included in mixed container plantings.

Recommended

R. acetosa (garden sorrel, broad leaf sorrel) is a vigorous, clump-forming perennial. The inconspicuous flowers are borne on a tall stem that emerges from the centre of the clump. This plant grows 45–90 cm (18–36") tall and spreads about 30 cm (12"). (Zones 4–8)

R. scutatus (French sorrel, buckler leaf sorrel) forms a low, slow-spreading clump of foliage. The leaves are stronger tasting but are not as plentiful as those of garden sorrel. This selection keeps its flavour better in warm weather than garden sorrel does. It grows 15–45 cm (6–18") tall and spreads up to 60 cm (24"). (Zones 4–8)

Problems and Pests

Snails, slugs, rust and leaf spot can cause rare problems.

Soybeans

Glycine

Features: bushy annual; edible seeds **Height:** 30–60 cm (12–24")
Spread: 30–45 cm (12–18")

These beans have been popular for years in Asian countires. One
common preparation method involves simmering the beans in the pod
in salted water. The seeds are then eaten out of the pods. The seeds
are also excellent roasted.

Starting

Sow seeds directly into the garden after the last frost date has passed and the soil has warmed up.

Growing

Soybeans grow best in **full sun,** but they tolerate some light afternoon shade. The soil should be of **average fertility** and **well drained**.

Harvesting

Harvest the beans when the pods are plump and full but the seeds are still tender and green. The pods can also be grown to maturity and the beans dried for use in soups and stews.

Tips

Soybeans are very ornamental, with attractive leaves and plentiful flowers. They can be used to make low, temporary hedges or planted in small groups in the border.

Recommended

G. max is a bushy annual that produces clusters of large-seeded pods. There are several available soybean cultivars, including **'Beer Friend,' 'Black Jet,' 'Manitoba Brown'** and **'Manitoba Butter Soy.'**

Problems and Pests

Leaf spot, bacterial blight, rust, bean beetles and aphids can cause problems.

Soybeans contain all nine essential amino acids, have no cholesterol and are low in saturated fats and sodium. They are an excellent source of dietary fibre and are high in iron, calcium, B vitamins, zinc, lecithin, phosphorous and magnesium.

Spinach
Spinacia

Features: clump-forming annual; smooth or crinkled edible leaves
Height: 30–45 cm (12–18") **Spread:** 15–25 cm (6–10")

Nutritious and versatile, spinach is useful in a wide variety of dishes. And it's effortless to grow, so you might want to consider adding this popular leafy plant to your garden, even if you don't grow any other vegetables. Spinach is particularly fond of maritime conditions.

Starting

Direct sow spinach in spring as soon as the soil can be worked. A young plant can tolerate a light frost, but if temperatures are expected to fall below -5° C (23° F) you should cover it. Several successive sowings in spring and again in mid- to late summer will provide you with a steady supply of tender leaves.

Growing

Spinach grows well in **full sun** or **light shade** and prefers cool weather and a cool location. The soil should be **fertile, moist** and **well drained**. Add a layer of mulch to help keep soil cool, because this plant bolts in hot weather. Many Canadian gardeners won't have to worry about bolting, because our cool summer nights are ideal for growing spinach. Bolt-resistant varieties are also available.

Harvesting

Pick leaves, as needed, a few at a time from each plant. The flavour tends to deteriorate as the weather heats up and the plant matures and goes to flower.

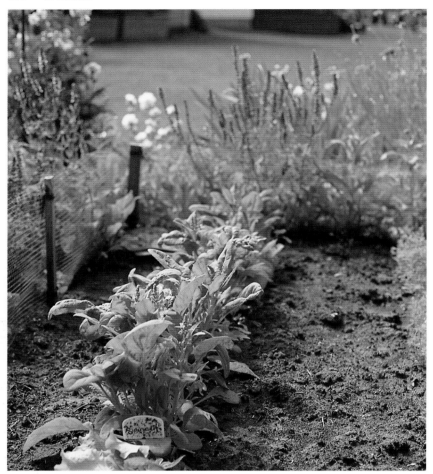

The unrelated New Zealand spinach (Tetragonia expansa) is an excellent and interesting alternative to regular spinach. The leaves can be used in the same way, but the plant is far more heat resistant, grows upright and branching in habit and can be planted in summer, as regular spinach begins to fade. It will grow quickly in the heat of summer and be ready for a late summer and autumn harvest.

Tips

Spinach's dark green foliage is attractive when mass planted and provides a good contrast for brightly coloured annual and perennial flowers. Try it in a mixed container that you keep close to an entryway to make harvesting more convenient.

Recommended

S. oleracea forms a dense, bushy clump of glossy dark green, smooth or crinkled (savoyed) foliage. Plants are ready for harvest in about 45 days. **'Bloomsdale'** produces dark green, deeply savoyed foliage. Many strains of this cultivar are also available. **'Correnta'** is a smooth-leaved variety with tender, dark green leaves. **'Scarlet'** is a smooth-leaved variety with dark red veins. **'Tyee'** is a semi-savoy variety that is very bolt resistant.

Problems and Pests

Avoid powdery and downy mildew by keeping a bit of space between each plant to allow for good air flow.

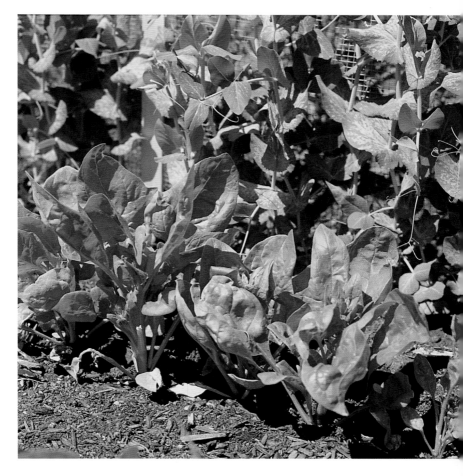

Squash

Cucurbita

Features: trailing or mounding annual; large lobed, decorative leaves; colourful flowers and fruit **Height:** 45–60 cm (18–24") **Spread:** 60 cm–3 m (2–10')

Squash are generally grouped as summer squash and winter squash. The groupings reflect when we eat the squash more than any real difference in the plants themselves. All squash develop hardened rinds in autumn if left to mature. The squash that keep the longest and have the best flesh taste and texture when mature are grouped as winter squash. Summer squash are tender and tasty when they are immature but tend to become stringy and sometimes bitter when they mature, and they don't keep as well.

Starting

Start seeds in peat pots indoors six to eight weeks before the last frost date. Keep them in as bright a location as possible to reduce stretching. Plant out or direct sow after the last frost date and once the soil has warmed up. Plant on mounds of soil to ensure there is good drainage away from the base of the plant.

Growing

Squash grow best in **full sun,** but tolerate light shade from companion plants. The soil should be **fertile, humus rich, moist** and **well drained**. Mulch well to keep the soil moist. Put mulch or straw under developing fruit of pumpkins and other heavy winter squash to protect the skin while it is tender. Squash generally need a long, warm summer to develop well. Gardeners in cooler areas will want to choose species and cultivars that mature in a shorter season.

Harvesting

Summer squash are tastiest when picked and eaten young. The more you pick, the more the plants will produce. Cut the fruit cleanly from the plant, and avoid damaging the leaves and stems to prevent disease and insect problems.

C. moschata (below)

C. pepo (above & below)

Winter squash should be harvested carefully, to avoid damaging the skins, just before the first hard frost. Allow them to cure in a warm, dry place for a few weeks until the skins become thick and hard. They can then be stored in a cool dry place where they will keep all winter. Check them regularly to be sure they aren't spoiling.

Tips

Mound-forming squash, with their tropical-looking leaves, can be added to borders as feature plants. Small-fruited, trailing selections can be grown up trellises. The heavy-fruited, trailing types will wind happily through a border of taller plants or shrubs. All squash can be grown in containers, but the mound-forming and shorter-trailing selections are usually most attractive; the long-trailing types end up as a stem that leads over the edge of the container.

Recommended
Squash plants are generally similar in appearance, with medium to large leaves held on long stems.

Plants are trailing in habit, but some form only very short vines so they appear to be more mound forming. Bright yellow, trumpet-shaped male and female flowers are borne separately but on the same plant. Female flowers can be distinguished by their short stem and by the juvenile fruit at the base of the flower. Male flowers have longer stems.

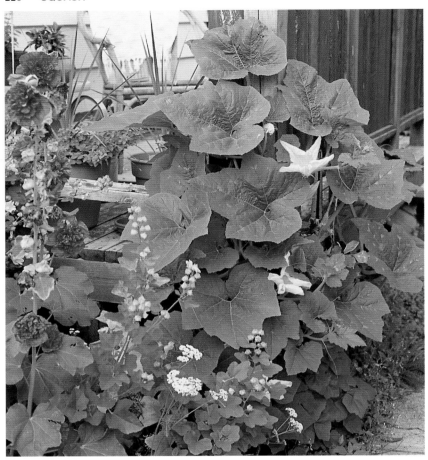

There are four species of squash commonly grown in gardens. They vary incredibly in their appearance and can be smooth or warty, round, elongated or irregular. In colour, they can be dark green, tan, creamy white or bright orange, and can be solid, stripy or spotted. The size ranges from tiny, round zucchini that would fit in the palm of a child's hand to immense pumpkins that could hold two or three children. Experiment with different types to find which ones grow best in your garden and which ones you like best.

C. maxima includes buttercup squash and hubbard. These plants generally need 90–110 days to mature. They keep very well, often longer than any other squash, and have sweet, fine-textured flesh.

C. mixta includes cushaw squash and is not as well known. These plants generally take 100 days or more to mature. Some are grown for their edible seeds, while others are used in baking and are good for muffins, loaves and pies.

C. moschata includes butternut squash and generally needs 95 or more days to mature. These squash keep well and are popular baked or for soups and stews.

C. pepo is the largest group of squash and includes summer squash, such as zucchini, and many winter squash, such as pumpkins, acorn squash, spaghetti squash, dumpling squash and gourds. Summer squash are ready to harvest in 45–50 days, and the winter squash in this group take from 70–75 days for acorn and spaghetti squash to 95–120 days for some of the larger pumpkins.

C. pepo (photos this page), female flower (above)

Problems and Pests
Problems with mildew, cucumber beetles, stem borers, bacterial wilt and whiteflies can occur. Ants may snack on damaged plants and fruit, and mice will eat and burrow into squash for the seeds in fall.

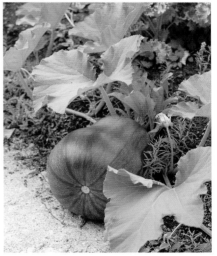

Don't worry if some of your summer squash are too mature or your winter squash are not mature enough. Summer squash can be cured and will keep for a couple of months. They are still useful for muffins and loaves. Immature winter squash can be harvested and used right away; try them stuffed, baked or barbecued.

Strawberries

Fragraria

Features: spreading perennial; soft, bright green leaves; white, sometimes pink flowers; bright red, edible fruit. **Height:** 15–30 cm (6–12") **Spread:** 30 cm (12"), or more

Many of these plants, with their pretty little white flowers, spread vigorously by runners. Long shoots spread out from the parent plant, and small baby plants grow at the tips. Purchasing just a few plants will quickly provide you with plenty of fruit-producing plants by the end of summer.

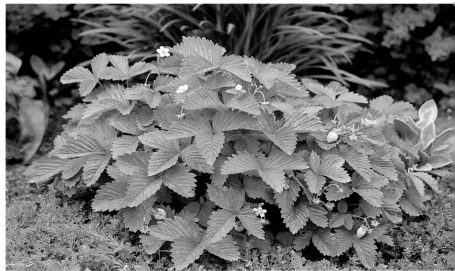

F. vesca (above)

Starting
Some selections can be started indoors about 12 weeks before you plan to plant them outside. Other selections are only available as crowns or plants. Plant them outdoors around the last frost date. They tolerate light frosts.

Growing
Strawberries grow well in **full sun** or **light shade**. The soil should be **fertile, neutral to alkaline, moist** and **well drained**. They tolerate acidic soil but don't produce as much fruit.

Harvesting
Pick strawberries as soon as they are ripe. Some types produce a single large crop of fruit in early summer, and others produce a smaller crop throughout most or all of summer.

Tips
Strawberries make interesting, tasty and quick-growing groundcovers. They do well in containers, window boxes and hanging baskets. The selections that don't produce runners are also good for edging beds.

Recommended
F. chiloensis (Chilean strawberry), *F. vesca* (wild strawberry, alpine strawberry) and *F. virginiana* (Virginia strawberry) have been crossed to form many hybrids. Similar in appearance, they generally form a low clump of three-part leaves and may or may not produce runners. Flowers in spring are followed by early to mid-summer fruit. Some plants produce a second crop in autumn, and others produce fruit all summer. Fruit of wild or alpine strawberries is smaller than the fruit of the other two species. Popular cultivars include mid-season producers **'Cabot'** and **'Kent'** and ever-bearing producers **'Sweetheart,' 'Temptation'** and **'Tristar.'** (Zones 3–8)

Problems and Pests
The fruit is susceptible to fungal diseases, so mulch to protect it. Some leaf spot, spider mite and wilt can occur.

Sunflower · Sunchoke

Helianthus

Features: daisy-like, yellow, orange, red, brown, cream or bicoloured flowers, typically with brown, purple or rusty red centres; edible seeds; edible tubers
Height: 1.8–4.5 m (6–15') **Spread:** 30–120 cm (12–48")

Sunflowers make wonderful companions for other seed-bearing plants such as amaranth and quinoa. Sunchokes are a native species that develop edible tubers, which taste like artichokes, radishes or waterchestnuts, depending on who is describing the flavour.

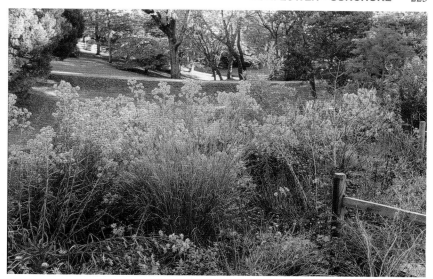

Starting

Sunflowers and sunchokes can be sown directly into the garden in spring around the last frost date. Water well until the plants become established. Sunchokes are perennial and will grow back each year as long as you leave some of the tubers in place in autumn.

Growing

Sunflowers and sunchokes grow best in **full sun**. The soil should be of **average fertility, humus rich, moist** and **well drained,** though plants adapt to a variety of conditions. They become quite drought tolerant as summer progresses.

Harvesting

Sunflower seeds are ready to harvest when the flower has withered and the seeds are plump. You may need to cover the flowerheads with a paper bag or net to prevent birds from eating all the seeds before you get to them.

Sunchoke tubers are usually ready to harvest around the time of the first frost in fall. They should be stored in a cool, dry, well-ventilated area.

Tips

Sunflowers make a striking addition to the back of the border and along fences and walls. These tall plants may need staking in windy or exposed locations.

Sunchokes can be boiled, baked, fried, steamed, stewed or eaten raw. They cook more quickly than potatoes do and become mushy if overcooked.

Recommended

H. annuum can develop a single stem or many branches. The large-flowered sunflowers usually develop a single stem. Many of the ornamental sunflowers offered in gardening catalogues have edible seeds. **'Russian Mammoth,'** a tall cultivar with large yellow flowers, is one of the most popular for seed production.

Sunflowers are a great way to invite birds into your garden if you don't mind not having the seeds for yourself. The birds will feast on garden pests as well as the seeds the flowers provide.

H. annuum (photos this page)

H. tuberosus (sunchoke, Jerusalem artichoke) is a tall, bushy, tuberous perennial. It grows 1.8–3.0 m (6–10') tall and spreads 60–120 cm (24–48"). Bright yellow flowers are produced in late summer and autumn. (Zones 2–8)

Problems and Pests
Plants are generally problem free, but keeping birds away from the seeds until they are ready to be picked can be troublesome.

Sunchokes store energy in the tubers as a carbohydrate called inulin, rather than starch. They are filling, but the energy is not readily absorbed by the body and does not affect blood sugar levels, making these tubers useful for diabetics and people who are trying to lose weight .

Tarragon

Artemisia

Features: narrow, fragrant leaves; airy flowers **Height:** 45–90 cm (18–36")
Spread: 30–45 cm (12–18")

The distinctive licorice-like flavour of tarragon lends itself to a wide variety of meat and vegetable dishes and is the key flavouring in Bernaise sauce.

Before purchasing a plant, chew a leaf to see if it has the distinct flavour it should have. French tarragon is preferred, whereas Russian tarragon (A. d. var. dracunculoides) is a more vigorous plant but has little of the desired flavour.

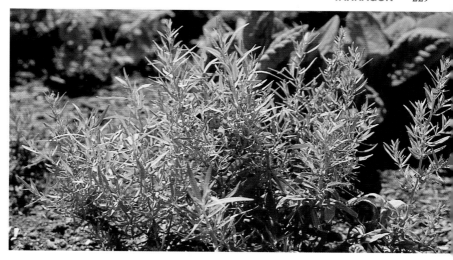

Starting

The tastiest tarragon is French tarragon, and it can only be propagated vegetatively. Seeds do not come true to type. Plants can be purchased at nurseries and garden centres and from specialty growers.

Growing

Tarragon grows best in **full sun**. The soil should be **average to fertile, moist** and **well drained**. Divide the plant every few years to keep it vigorous and encourage the best leaf flavour.

Harvesting

Pick leaves as needed to use fresh, and dry or freeze some in late summer for winter use.

Tips

Tarragon is not exceptionally decorative, but it does provide a good vertical presence. It can be included in an herb garden or mixed border, where the surrounding plants will support its tall stems.

Recommended

A. dracunculus var. *sativa* is a bushy plant with tall stems and narrow leaves. Airy clusters of insignificant flowers are produced in late summer. (Zones 3–8)

Problems and Pests

Tarragon rarely suffers from any problems.

Thyme
Thymus

Features: bushy habit; fragrant, decorative foliage; purple, pink or white summer flowers **Height:** 20–40 cm (8–16") **Spread:** 20–60 cm (8–24")

Thyme is a popular culinary herb used in the cooking of soups, stews, casseroles and roasts.

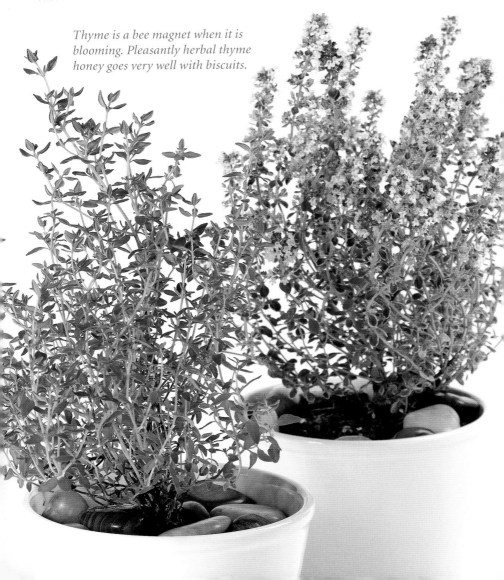

Thyme is a bee magnet when it is blooming. Pleasantly herbal thyme honey goes very well with biscuits.

Starting

Common thyme can be started indoors from seed four to six weeks before you plan to plant it outdoors. This plant can be purchased at nurseries and garden centres, and from specialty growers.

Growing

Thyme prefers **full sun**. The soil should be **neutral to alkaline** and of **poor to average fertility**. Good drainage is essential. It is beneficial to work leaf mould and sharp limestone gravel into the soil to improve structure and drainage.

Harvesting

Pick leaves as needed for fresh use or to dry for use in winter.

Tips

Thyme is useful for sunny, dry locations at the front of borders, between or beside paving stones, on rock walls and in containers. Once the plant has finished flowering, shear it back by about half to encourage new growth and to prevent it from becoming too woody.

Recommended

T. x *citriodorus* (lemon-scented thyme) forms a mound of lemon-scented, dark green foliage. The summer flowers are pale pink. Cultivars with silver- or gold-margined leaves are available.

T. vulgaris (common thyme) forms a bushy mound of fragrant, dark green leaves. The summer flowers may be purple, pink or white. Cultivars with variegated leaves are available.

Problems and Pests

Thyme rarely suffers from any problems, but its roots can rot in poorly drained, wet soils.

Tomatoes

Lycopersicon

Features: annual vine; bushy upright or trailing habit; fragrant foliage; yellow flowers; edible red, pink, orange or yellow fruit **Height:** 45 cm–1.5 m (18"–5') **Spread:** 45–90 cm (18–36")

Tomatoes are so wonderful fresh off the vine that I can't remember a summer when I didn't have a container of them growing on my balcony, front step, back porch or garden, no matter how small my apartment or accommodations were at the time.

Starting

Tomatoes can be started indoors six to eight weeks before the last frost date or can be purchased in spring from nurseries and garden centres.

Growing

Tomatoes grow best in **full sun**. The soil should be **average to fertile, humus rich, moist** and **well drained**. Keep tomatoes evenly moist to encourage good fruit production. Except for the very small bush selections, tomatoes tend to be quite tall and are prone to flopping over unless stakes, wire hoops, tomato cages or other supports are used.

Harvesting

Pick the fruit as soon as it is ripe. Tomatoes pull easily from the vine with a gentle twist when they are ready for picking.

Tips

Tomatoes are bushy and have both attractive little flower clusters and vibrantly coloured fruit. Many of the selections grow well in containers and are included in patio gardens and hanging baskets.

Recommended

L. lycopersicum are bushy or vine-forming annuals with pungent, bristly leaves and stems. Determinate plants grow a specific height and are generally short enough to not need staking. Indeterminate plants continue to grow all summer and usually need staking. Clusters of yellow flowers are followed by fruit from mid-summer through to the first frost. Fruit ripen to red, orange, pink or yellow and come in many shapes and sizes. Beefsteak tomatoes produce the largest fruit, and cherry tomatoes produce the smallest fruit. Browse through a seed catalogue to see the many offerings available. Try a few each year until you find your favourites.

When tomatoes plants were first introduced to Europe, they were grown as ornamental plants, not for their edible fruit.

Problems and Pests
Problems with tobacco mosaic
virus, aphids, fungal wilt, blossom
end rot and nematodes can occur.

*Tomatillos (Physalis ixocarpa) are
related to tomatoes, and the plants
have similar cultural requirements.
The fruit is encased in a delicate
papery husk. It is ready to pick when
the husk is loose and the fruit has
turned from green to gold or light
brown.*

Turnip

Brassica

Features: biennial, grown as an annual; clump of edible, blue-green foliage; plump, edible root **Height:** 25–45 cm (10–18") **Spread:** 15–20 cm (6–8")

Tender with a delicate flavour, turnips should be eaten as soon as they mature for the best-tasting roots.

Turnips, originally grown as animal fodder, only became popular for dinner in the 1600s.

B. rapa (above & below)

Starting
Sow seeds directly into the garden in spring. Keep the seedbed moist until plants germinate. Several smaller successive sowings will provide you with turnips for longer.

Growing
Turnips prefer to grow in **full sun**. The soil should be **fertile, acidic, moist** and **well drained**. The roots can develop discoloured centres if the soil is boron deficient; agricultural boron can be worked into the soil if needed.

Harvesting
The leaves can be harvested a few at a time from each plant as needed and steamed or added to stir-fries. The roots should be harvested as soon as they are plump, because they have the best flavour and texture when young. Turnips do not keep well when stored.

Tips
These plants form attractive clumps of foliage and can be added in small groups to borders where the foliage provides a good background for flowering plants.

Recommended
B. rapa (turnip, summer turnip) is a biennial, grown as an annual. It produces edible, white or purple-shouldered roots. The blue-green foliage is also edible. **'Early Purple Top White Globe'** and **'White Lady'** are popular cultivars.

Problems and Pests
Cabbage root maggots, cabbage white butterfly larvae, aphids, rust, fungal diseases, downy mildew, powdery mildew and clubroot are possible problems.

Watermelon

Citrullus

Features: annual vines; climbing or trailing habit; decorative fruit; yellow flowers; dark green striped, pale green skinned fruit **Height:** 30 cm (12") **Spread:** 1.5–3 m (5–10')

Tasty and juicy, watermelon is the ultimate summer treat. Make it an even bigger treat and try growing your own. It grows best in hot, humid weather, but plenty of short-season varieties are available for Canadian gardeners.

Starting

Watermelon requires a long growing season and should be started indoors in individual peat pots four to six weeks before the last frost date. Started plants can also be purchased at garden centres and nurseries. Transplant them into the garden after the last frost date and once the soil has warmed up.

Growing

Watermelon grows best in **full sun**. The soil should be **fertile, humus rich, moist** and **well drained**. It likes plenty of water during the growth and early fruiting stages but, to intensify the flavour, should be allowed to dry out a bit once the fruit is ripening.

Harvesting

A watermelon is generally ready to pick when the pale white area on the skin, where the fruit sits, turns yellow. Some experimentation may be required before you become adept at judging the ripeness of the fruit.

Tips

The small-fruited watermelon makes an attractive patio climber, though the small fruit may need some support as it grows. This plant can be left to wind through ornamental beds and borders.

Recommended

C. lanatus takes 65–105 days to mature; the skin of the fruit may be light green with dark green stripes or solid dark green; the flesh may be red, pink, orange or yellow. Popular, early maturing cultivars include **'Gypsy,' 'New Queen,' 'Sugar Baby'** and **'Yellow Doll.'**

Problems and Pests

Problems with powdery mildew, *fusarium* wilt, cucumber beetles and sap beetles can occur. Watermelon fruit blotch is a serious problem that can affect this plant, but it has not been found in Canada.

Watermelon is native to tropical parts of Africa, but it was introduced to Asia and has been grown there for centuries.

Glossary

Acid soil: soil with a pH lower than 7.0

Alkaline soil: soil with a pH higher than 7.0

Annual: a plant that germinates, flowers, sets seeds and dies in one growing season

Basal leaves: leaves that form from the crown, at the base of the plant

Blanching: to deprive a plant or part of a plant of light, resulting in a pale colour and usually a milder flavour

Bolting: when a plant produces flowers and seeds prematurely, usually rendering the plant inedible

Bract: a special, modified leaf at the base of a flower or inflorescence; bracts may be small or large, green or coloured

Cross-pollination: the pollination of one plant by a closely related one. Undesirable if the resulting seeds or fruit lack the expected qualities; beneficial if an improved variety results

Crown: the part of the plant at or just below soil level where the shoots join the roots

Cultivar: a cultivated plant variety with one or more distinct differences from the species, e.g., in flower colour or disease resistance

Damping off: fungal disease causing seedlings to rot at soil level

Deadhead: removing spent flowers to maintain a neat appearance and encourage a long blooming season

Diatomaceous earth: an abrasive dust made from the fossilized remains of diatoms, a species of algae; the scratches it makes on insect bodies allows internal fluids to leak out and the insects die of dehydration

Direct sow: to sow seeds directly into the garden

Dormancy: a period of plant inactivity, usually during winter or unfavourable conditions

Double flower: a flower with an unusually large number of petals

Drought resistant: can withstand drought for a long time

Drought tolerant: can withstand drought conditions, but only for a limited time

Genus: a category of biological classification between the species and family levels; the first word in a scientific name indicates the genus

Half-hardy: a plant capable of surviving the climatic conditions of a given region if protected from heavy frost or cold

Harden off: to gradually acclimatize plants that have been growing in a protected environment to a harsher environment

Hardy: capable of surviving unfavourable conditions, such as cold weather or frost, without protection

Humus: decomposed or decomposing organic material in the soil

Hybrid: a plant resulting from natural or human-induced cross-breeding between varieties, species or genera

Inflorescence: an arrangement of flowers on a single stem

Invasive: able to spread aggressively and outcompete other plants

Loam: a loose soil composed of clay, sand and organic matter, often highly fertile

Microclimate: an area of beneficial or detrimental growing conditions within a larger area

Mulch: a material (e.g., shredded bark, pine cones, leaves, straw), used to surround a plant to protect it from weeds, cold or heat and to promote moisture retention

Neutral soil: soil with a pH of 7.0

Node: the area on a stem from which a leaf or new shoot grows

Perennial: a plant that takes three or more years to complete its life cycle

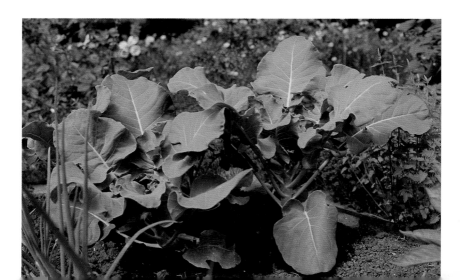

pH: a measure of acidity or alkalinity; soil pH influences availability of nutrients for plants

Plantlet: a young or small plant

Potager: an ornamental kitchen garden, often laid out symmetrically with raised beds or low hedge-edged beds

Rhizome: a root-like, food-storing stem that grows horizontally at or just below soil level, from which new shoots may emerge

Rosette: a low, flat cluster of leaves arranged like the petals of a rose

Runner: a modified stem that grows on the soil surface; roots and new shoots are produced at nodes along its length

Seedhead: dried, inedible fruit that contains seeds

Self-seeding: reproducing by means of seeds without human assistance, so that new plants constantly replace those that die

Single flower: a flower with a single ring of typically four or five petals

Spathe: a leaf-like bract that encloses a flower cluster or spike

Species: the fundamental unit of biological classification; the entity from which cultivars and varieties are derived

Standard: a tree or shrub pruned to form a rounded head of branches at the top of a clearly visible stem

Subspecies (subsp.): a naturally occurring, often regional, form of a species, isolated from other subspecies but still potentially interfertile with them

Taproot: a root system consisting of one long main root with smaller roots or root hairs branching from it

Tender: incapable of surviving the climatic conditions of a given region and requiring protection from frost or cold

Tuber: the thick section of a rhizome bearing nodes and buds

Understorey plant: a plant that prefers to grow beneath the canopies of trees in a woodland setting

Variegation: foliage that has more than one colour, often patched, striped or bearing leaf margins of a different colour

Variety (var.): a naturally occurring variant of a species

Index of Plant Names

Boldface type refers to the primary species accounts

248

Acknowledgements

To my good friend Cherie Demers, who lets me plant my extras in her garden, where they invariably do better than in mine, and to my dearest Robin, who always wants more edible things planted and so, in part, inspired this book. I'd also like to thank my gardening colleagues Don Williamson, Laura Peters and Heather Markham and everyone at Lone Pine for their constant hard work.

Photography Credits

All photos by Laura Peters, except: All American Selections 159b; Joan de Grey 199b; Frank De Meyer 37a, 89a; Tamara Eder 6a, 10, 31c, 32b, 35b, 35c, 39a, 42a, 42b, 47b, 43, 80, 179a, 179b, 181a, 181b, 207a; Elliot Engley 26a, 26b, 26c, 27a, 27b; Jen Fafard 119a, 227a; Derek Fell 12a, 15b, 32a, 36a, 37b, 38a, 38b, 54a, 55a, 57a, 58, 59a, 59b, 62, 63a, 65, 76, 77a, 78, 79, 84b, 85a, 92, 93, 95, 103, 104a, 104b, 105, 109a, 110a, 127a, 127b, 135a, 137a, 141b, 142, 143, 144a, 151a, 154, 155, 159a, 161a, 161b, 163b, 165b, 167a, 167b, 177a, 177b, 178b, 179c, 205, 211a, 211b, 216, 217b, 218b, 237b; Erica Flatt 11a; Saxon Holt 7b, 67, 107a, 225a; Liz Klose 8, 13, 18a, 34s, 40a, 40b, 49, 57b, 71a, 77b, 83, 84a, 88, 111b, 114, 115, 125, 129a, 135b, 139a, 169b, 174a, 183b, 195b, 203a, 219, 233b; Trina Koscielnuk 108; Olga Langerova 197b; L. Lauzuma 197a; Scott Leigh 101; Janet Loughrey 71b, 200b; Heather Markham 47c; Tim Matheson 7a, 15a, 17a, 18b, 19a, 19b, 19c, 19d, 20, 21a, 21b, 24b, 24c, 27c, 32c, 36b, 41a, 41b, 45, 46, 47a, 48, 107b, 225b, 226a, 226b, 227b, 227c; Marilyn McAra 162a; Liza McCorkle 89b; Photos.com 28c, 35a, 96, 99a, 99b, 239; Robert Ritchie 39b; Nanette Samol 4, 9, 23a, 24d, 25b, 30, 31a, 31b, 34b, 50, 52, 56, 60, 64, 66, 68, 72, 81, 82, 86, 90, 94, 100, 102, 106, 112, 116, 120, 124, 126, 128, 130, 132, 134, 138, 140, 146, 150, 151b, 152, 156, 157a, 157b, 158, 164, 166, 168, 170, 172, 176, 178a, 180, 182, 186, 188a, 188b, 189a, 190, 194, 198, 202, 204, 206, 208, 210, 212, 222, 224, 228, 229b, 232, 236, 238, 151b, 157a, 157b, 160, 178a, 188a, 188b, 189a; Don Williamson 17b.